HOUSE vs. SENATE

CONFLICT IN THE APPROPRIATIONS PROCESS

HOUSE
vs.
SENATE

CONFLICT IN THE
APPROPRIATIONS PROCESS

JEFFREY L. PRESSMAN

NEW HAVEN AND LONDON, YALE UNIVERSITY PRESS, 1966

FOR MY FAMILY

The tradition of undergraduate writing and publishing has long been a very lively one at Yale, as witnessed by the large number of periodicals, journalistic or literary in character, which have appeared on the Yale campus. These, however, fail to give an accurate picture of the high proportion of good and original scholarly writing which is also done by undergraduates. The excellence of many of the Honors theses written by Yale Seniors made it desirable some years ago to give the most deserving of them the circulation which publication in printed form could provide. Between 1941 and 1957 ten volumes were published in the Undergraduate Prize Essays Series and two in the Scholars of the House Series. The authors of several of these essays have gone on to fulfill amply the promise of their early scholarly efforts. More recently the growing number of theses of outstanding merit has encouraged Yale College and the Yale University Press to establish this new Yale College Series with the hope that every year it will be possible to publish some of the best work by the Honors majors in the Senior Class. The selection, which is necessarily a very rigorous one, was performed for the Class of 1965 by a faculty committee made up of Messrs. S. W. Reed, M. I. J. Griffin, and E. M. Waith, Chairman.

Georges May
Dean of Yale College

FOREWORD

There is a fairly widespread suspicion among those who observe the annual battle of the budget that the appropriations process in Congress is not all that it ought to be. In recent years members of Congress, journalists, and scholars have all advanced proposals of one kind or another to change the appropriations process.

These reforms run swiftly into major obstacles—genuine obstacles of the kind that not infrequently face any attempt to change an active and powerful institution. To begin with, only a very small number of people in Congress or outside it know much about the process. In a very brief space of time, anyone can familiarize himself with the elementary facts about nuclear fission; so too with appropriations. But in both cases the process is so intricate that knowledge merely of the superficial facts does not lead to much understanding.

Those who know the intricate details best are doubtless the members of Congress who serve on the appropriations committees of House and Senate. By the time they have mastered these details, however, they are likely to have acquired a considerable interest in keeping the process the way it is, a strong belief that not much can be done to change it, and a well-founded disdain for proposals made by outsiders who do not seem to understand the realities within which decision-making in Congress takes place.

Anyone who wishes to understand the process must surely do as Mr. Pressman has done: he must immerse himself in the details and the views of the process that only the members of the appropriations committees and their staffs can furnish him. But details do not necessarily provide much in the way of perspective; like the member of Congress, the reflective outsider may find himself torn between alternative ways of judging the process. Thus what seems most obvious to an observer is how little opportunity there is for any member of Congress, including the Senators and Representatives serving on the appropriations committees, ever to have an overview of the budget; the Senators or Representatives are lost in details. It is tempting, therefore, to design reforms that would appear to provide Congress with a greater opportunity to see the budget whole and less opportunity to bog down in details. Critics with a different perspective object, however, that such reforms are very likely to provide an illusion of rationality and yet lead inevitably to wildly irrational behavior on the part of Congress. For who can intelligently decide without knowing many of the details whether, let us say, foreign aid should amount to $3 million or $9 billion? Congressional experience lends solid support to these critics. If it is said that one should leave matters to the executive branch, one is in effect arguing that the British parliamentary system should be adopted on the budget—but without the safeguards of that system.

In much the same way, the observer may be caught between differing perspectives about the value of conflict. It seems obvious that conflict between House and Senate over appropriations is sometimes costly and unproductive, particularly when it leads to deadlock and the failure to make any appropriations at all in time for the agencies to start the new fiscal year. However much battles over prestige and power may contribute to the well-being or distress of Representatives and Senators, as citizens we may well feel that this particular game is expensive and unnecessary to *our* well-being. Nonetheless, the American political system is founded on a principle that in recent years a number of social scientists have come to insist on emphatically: conflict is often desirable too. But how much conflict and of what kinds? There are the difficult problems. If it is useful, for example, to have some conflict over appropriations between Executive and Congress or between spenders whose eyes are on the benefits of programs and penny-pinchers who are looking at the costs, how much and of what kinds?

One of the many merits of Mr. Pressman's book is that he does not look at the appropriations process out of one eye. He is highly sensitive to the complexities of the appropriations process itself, its institutional setting, and problems of appraising alternatives. He is properly wary of simplistic diagnoses and prescriptions for reform. Because his study is informed, thoughtful, and judicious, his own proposal for the creation of a conference committee staff merits very serious attention from everyone, whether Senator, Representative, journalist, or scholar, who is interested in improving the appropriations process in Congress.

May 11, 1966   Robert A. Dahl

ACKNOWLEDGMENTS

While engaged in writing this essay for the Yale College Intensive Program in Political Science, I was fortunate to have the helpful criticism and understanding guidance of Professors Herbert Kaufman, William K. Muir, Jr., and Irwin Gertzog. Dr. Muir instructed me in the use of social theory, and Professors Kaufman and Gertzog helped me to understand the subtleties of congressional behavior. Also extremely helpful in the difficult early stages of preparation was Professor Richard F. Fenno, Jr., of the University of Rochester, whose article on the House Appropriations Committee had first stimulated my interest in internal committee politics. Outside the academic world, summer internships with Senators Lee Metcalf and George McGovern gave me an opportunity to talk to legislators about their appropriations work and to observe Congress from the inside.

I am indebted to the seven members of the Senate Appropriations Committee (three Democrats and four Republicans) and the nine members of the House committee (six Democrats and three Republicans), who granted interviews averaging approximately forty-five minutes in length. Included in the Senate interviews were three with subcommittee chairmen; included on the House side was one with a subcommittee chairman. Five Senate committee staff members and two House committee staff members also agreed to be interviewed. Because of the confidential nature of the interviews, the legislators and staff members asked that their names not be used. Therefore, the source of a direct quotation will be identified as "a Senate subcommittee chairman," "a House staff member," etc.

Since the 1962 conflict between the Senate and House Appropriations Committees is a focal point of the study, all of the people interviewed were asked to give an assessment of that conflict. They were then asked about the causes of appropriations battles—why, for example, does the Senate committee usually recommend a higher appropriations figure than does its opposite number in the House? Finally, the senators, representatives, and staff members were asked to evaluate the consequences of conflict and to state the ways, if any, in which they thought the appropriations process might be improved. In addition to this general questioning, individual congressmen and aides were asked to describe House–Senate relations in their own particular subject areas and to reconstruct events which had taken place in interhouse conferences in which they had been participants.

After the essay had been completed, Professors David Danelski and Hayward R. Alker, Jr., of the Yale Political Science Department offered helpful comments concerning both political interpretation and style. Professors Stephen W. Reed and Eugene M. Waith of the Yale College Series Committee suggested a number of revisions which would help to turn an undergraduate thesis into a book, and Ruth L. Davis of the Yale University Press, who supervised the final preparation of the manuscript for publication, made this process a surprisingly pleasant one.

Above all, I would like to thank Professor Robert A. Dahl, who served as my adviser in the writing of this essay. From the time that I burst into his office in my Junior year, wanting to write on "something to do with Congress," through the process of rewriting, Professor Dahl was always as generous with his advice as he was demanding in the standards he set. Without his help, the book might still have been written —but the writing of it would not have been nearly so exciting an experience.

J. L. P.

Oxford
January 1966

CONTENTS

I

"TWO OLD MEN"

The octogenarians' deadlock, which is blocking billions of dollars in appropriations on Capitol Hill, held fast today despite peace maneuvers.
    Robert Trussell, *in* The New York Times,
    June 19, 1962.

Two years ago, the seniority system permitted two octogenarians, Sen. Carl Hayden (D–Ariz.) and Clarence Cannon (D–Mo.) to hold up all appropriations bills for three months because they wouldn't agree on which would walk across the Capitol to meet the other . . . They were pleasant, able men, but seniority had gone to their heads.
    Drew Pearson's *Washington Merry-Go-Round,*
    December 9, 1964.

In 1962, a year-long feud between the Senate and House Appropriations Committees kept Congress in turmoil through much of the legislative season. Numerous reporters and columnists painted the feud as a lively personal battle between octogenarians: Representative Clarence Cannon (83), Chairman of the House Appropriations Committee, and Senator Carl Hayden (84), Chairman of the Senate Appropriations Committee. In a memorable cartoon by Poinier in the *Detroit News,* Cannon and Hayden are seated in wheel

1

chairs which have been placed back-to-back. "Water Guns at Ten Paces," shouts Hayden as he brandishes a toy pistol and rides away on his chair. If the prevailing picture of the 1962 battle as merely an octogenarians' feud were accurate, then there would be little need to carry on a deeper study of the conflict between committees. It is therefore extremely important to evaluate carefully the "two old men" argument.

The dispute centered on these questions: Does the Senate have the right under the Constitution to initiate appropriations in bills of its own? May the Senate add to House-passed appropriations measures funds for items not previously considered by the House, or considered and turned down? Where should Senate–House conference committees on appropriations meet and by whom should they be chaired?

The Constitution, I(7), requires that "All bills for raising revenue shall originate in the House of Representatives." By tradition, this has been true of appropriations bills also. Appropriations bills originate in one of the twelve subcommittees of the fifty-member House Appropriations Committee and recommendations are usually accepted without change by the full House. After House passage, each bill is referred to the Senate Appropriations Committee, which consists of twenty-seven members and thirteen subcommittees. The Senate subcommittees hold brief hearings, and the House-approved funds are usually increased in the Senate. Following Senate passage, the bill goes to conference— historically held on the Senate side of the Capitol and presided over by a Senate conferee. The final amount adopted is usually a compromise between Senate and House figures.

If appropriations legislation for the new fiscal year has not been completed by July 1, it is necessary for the two houses to adopt some kind of emergency legislation to enable the government agencies to continue operations on a daily basis. This is usually done by joint resolution.

CHRONOLOGY OF CONFLICT: 1962

In April, the House committee adopted a resolution calling for rotation between the Senate and House sides of the Capitol as sites for conferences on appropriations bills. (Appropriations conferences had traditionally been held on the Senate side.) The Senate countered with a proposal that the upper house originate one half of all appropriations bills. As a result, a conference did not meet until July—and failure to act held up appropriations. On June 14, the House appropriated $133,259,929 in supplemental funds. Hayden considered this sum inadequate, and told Cannon so. Then the aging Senate chairman offered to arrange a meeting in the Old Supreme Court Chamber, halfway between the Senate and the House. After demanding that the chairman of the conference should be a House member one half of the time, Representative Cannon injected a new issue into the affair: the "economy issue." According to Cannon, the higher Senate appropriations figures indicated that senators were profligate spenders.

Attacking the House emergency bill as inadequate, the Senate passed an expanded version of the measure on June 23. Senate Democratic leader Mike Mansfield suggested that the whole question of Senate–House conferences be examined. In the eyes of Mr. Mansfield, the deepening conflict had dangerous implications. Not only would it mean payless paydays for government employees, he said, but also it could spread through the economy and throw thousands of persons out of work if defense contract payments were not made.[1]

Faced with the unpleasant consequences of inaction, the House committee on June 28 reported a new measure which was a temporary "continuing" resolution. Since no new

1. Associated Press story, *New York Times,* June 24, 1962.

3

projects may be started under such a resolution, projects like the U.S. pavilion at the World's Fair were left in abeyance. Meanwhile, the effects of the conflict were being felt throughout the government. On June 29, the *Times* reported that:

> The Secret Service, which is short of funds needed for paying agents protecting the President and his family, has been forced to request the agents involved to wait for two weeks of salaries. In the State Department, funds deficiencies have caused delays in placing Foreign Service officers at newly assigned outposts and other difficulties.[2]

During July, the two committees set up special five-man teams of negotiators to try to resolve the dispute. Senator Hayden appointed Senator Richard B. Russell, the Georgia Democrat, to head the Senate team. As his panel went to work, Mr. Russell said that the senators had "extended olive branches until they were tired." Two resolutions were drafted by the Russell group: one was a defiant refusal to change procedures; the second contended that Senator Hayden had been subjected to "vicious and unfair attack" by the press and other media during the deadlock.[3]

All the wrangling was too much for *Times* Washington correspondent Tom Wicker, who threw up his hands in dismay at the "congressional banana war." Wicker asked: "Is Congress approaching the limits of adaptability to changing circumstances that has been the genius of the American system of government?"[4] Noting the fact that two weeks of the fiscal year had elapsed without a dime having been appropriated for any agency, he saw the roots of this conflict in

2. C. P. Trussell, *New York Times,* June 29, 1962.
3. Trussell, *New York Times,* July 7, 1962.
4. *New York Times,* July 15, 1962.

the tremendous power of the chairmen and the increasing rivalry between the House and Senate. But Wicker did not merely identify the problems; he tried to solve them:

> Almost every advocate of Congressional reform points to the need for a Joint Appropriations Committee, rather than two separate committees repeating each other's work and making equal demands on the executive branch to justify its requests. A joint group would have made the Cannon–Hayden feud impossible, among other things.

Finally, on July 18, a temporary solution was found for the stalemate. The selection of conference chairmen for the remainder of the session would be left to the chairmen of the House and Senate subcommittees handling each bill. Furthermore, a joint committee was organized to study disputed issues.

This, however, was not the end of the conflict. A Senate–House dispute over agricultural research funds late in the session resulted in a deadlock on the Agriculture Department Appropriations Bill. On October 4 the Senate passed SJ Res. 234, continuing the agricultural appropriations for fiscal 1963 at fiscal 1962 level. At this point the House rebuked the Senate, asserting that the Senate could not initiate appropriations measures. Senators Russell and Morse were furious, and later that month the upper chamber adopted a resolution asserting its "coequal power" with the House to originate appropriations bills. After all, the senators reasoned, the Constitution only gives the House exclusive power in "raising revenue."

Now the stage was set for Clarence Cannon's final dramatic move. On October 12 he blocked action on the First Supplemental Appropriations Bill for fiscal 1963 by objecting to a unanimous consent request to send it to conference.

5

Cannon "wanted to discourage the habit of the Senate of adding unwarranted sums to House appropriations bills,"[5] and he was reported to be "angered at the Senate addition of some $4,280,000 in special projects."[6]

PERSONALITIES OR BASIC POWER RELATIONSHIP?

To *Times* reporter C. P. Trussell, the appropriations tangle was really "a long-run opera bouffe starring two congressional octogenarians."[7] Above Trussell's article on June 17 were pictures of Hayden and Cannon, scowling at the reader. But there were those who went further in their interpretations. In the July 14 *Christian Science Monitor*, Richard L. Strout dismissed the notion that the appropriations conflict was merely a battle of chairmen. "The fact is," said Strout, "that a big issue is involved: the power status of Senate and House."[8] And a *New York Times* editorial on July 15 explained how conflict had built up between the houses:

> There has always been some tension in the relations between the Senate, where the states still pretend to be sovereign and send ambassadors, and the House, which in a large and sketchy way is "representative." . . . The Senators . . . remain scarcer than Representatives and therefore, at least by their own construction, more valuable. . . . Under these circumstances there is bound to be pulling and hauling between the two houses of Congress just as there is between Congress as a whole and the administration. . . . Representatives who face the facts cannot help feeling more numerous than the Sen-

5. *Congressional Quarterly Almanac*, 1962, p. 146.
6. *Washington Post*, October 14, 1962.
7. *New York Times*, June 17, 1962.
8. *Christian Science Monitor*, July 14, 1962.

ators, but they don't *want* to be treated as less influential in public.

Since 1956, when he was first elected to the Senate, Joseph S. Clark has been a perceptive and critical analyst of the workings and leadership of Congress. In *Congress: The Sapless Branch,* published in 1964, Clark discusses the 1962 appropriations battle and the press coverage of it. "The press billed the dispute as one between the two octogenarians," Clark notes. "Actually, these two men are on personally friendly terms. The trouble lies far deeper."[9] According to Clark, many members of the House would like to turn the Senate into an impotent House of Lords. Senate resentment of this view is fierce, and every so often the battle breaks into the open.

The interpretation of the 1962 conflict as an isolated battle between two men weakens when records of the past fifteen years are studied. For the 1962 affair was only one of three major conflicts between the two bodies during that period. During the 1949 session, Congress was rocked by disagreement between the Senate and House over the size of the Air Force. A conference report on the defense appropriations bill was held up for over a month, and adjournment was delayed until October 19. At a time when the Cold War was becoming increasingly bitter, such a tieup in defense funds constituted a serious problem. (This disagreement cannot be attributed to personal animosity between Cannon and Hayden; neither man has specialized in defense matters. Besides, Senator McKellar was chairman of the Senate committee at that time.)

In 1961 an adjournment-eve conference battle broke out over first supplemental appropriations for fiscal 1962. Can-

9. Joseph S. Clark, *Congress: The Sapless Branch* (New York, Harper and Row, 1964), p. 133.

non and Hayden were not the major personalities involved in this case; the conflict concerned appropriations for the legislative branch of government. Senator A. S. Mike Monroney and Representative Tom Steed, both Oklahomans, were chairmen of the subcommittees involved. During the feud, Steed made headlines with his charge that senators were using their office funds to pay call girls. In an act of defiance, the House adjourned for the year before the Senate could take up the conference report. Now the members of the upper house found themselves in an uncomfortable dilemma: if they did not adopt the unwelcome House provisions, the bill would die and agencies would be cut off from funds. The measure was indeed a bitter pill for the Senate to swallow. For included in it were provisions for extending the representatives' mail franking privileges (a measure opposed by the Senate). Omitted from the bill was a House-opposed Senate amendment raising the senators' allowances for office staff.

Thus, it appears that the House–Senate appropriations conflict of 1962 was not an isolated phenomenon. Rather, as Senator Clark suggests, there is a continuing tension between the two committees which breaks into the open from time to time.

A View from the Inside

As helpful as newspaper accounts and historical records are, it was essential to talk to people who were intimately involved with the 1962 events. Therefore, interviews were arranged in April, July, and August 1964 with members of the Senate and House committees and their staffs. Each interviewee was asked at the outset about the nature of the 1962 conflict. Was it a showdown between octogenarians? A House staff member especially close to Mr. Cannon had this to say: "The press was wrong—this was *not* a fight between two old men. Something flowed from the whole committee. Two men were obliged to stand up for their respective committees. Cannon and Hayden were the best of friends." An assistant of Mr. Hayden's remarked that "there was nothing personal between Cannon and Hayden. The House is just jealous of its appropriations right." Of all the men interviewed, only one representative (a junior member of the committee) expressed the opinion that there *had* been a personal clash between the two crusty chairmen. Still, he conditioned his view: "Although this was a character conflict between two petulant men, there was an underlying issue. There was a basic dispute over the constitutional question. And, I might add, a great deal of animosity between the committees of the House and Senate."

But if the conflict is seen as growing from deeper issues which divide the committees, it must be admitted that the pugnacious Representative Cannon was a catalyst who helped to change latent hostility into open battle. The same cannot, however, be said of Senator Hayden. Interestingly enough, it appears that Hayden, far from carrying on a personal feud with Cannon, was not eager to press the issue. An important observation came from one of Hayden's subcommittee chairmen: "Hayden wasn't worked up about this at all. When he talked to his subcommittee chairmen, he urged restraint. But Dick Russell wasn't so ready to pull punches, and he kept sending Hayden back to fight against Cannon." This opinion was echoed by a Republican senator who warned that the battle would probably erupt again. "You have to divorce it from two old men—younger, more flexible men were behind all of this. Dick Russell, for instance, would have been a lot more forceful. He felt that the Senate should really force the issue."

Senator Richard B. Russell of Georgia was the leader of

9

the special Senate team which negotiated with the House during the conflict. And it was the Russell group's report that angrily chastised the press and advised a policy of no surrender. Furthermore, Senator Russell was the man who took the floor of the Senate to defend the upper chamber's constitutional claims. Thus, he was in the forefront of the Senate attack. If Senator Hayden were to relinquish the chairmanship of the committee, Senator Russell would be first in line to succeed him. The Senate committee under Russell's leadership might become much more aggressive, increasing the likelihood of future interhouse battles.

At any rate, a feeling of sharp animosity has grown up between the House and Senate Appropriations Committees. To the House committee members, senators are headline-hunters who do a careless job in the appropriations field. As one young congressman put it:

> The fifty members of the House Appropriations Committee are experts. They sift evidence and studiously tackle appropriations. The Senate knows nothing. They have little time and do not go into the evidence. In conferences, they don't contribute much. You have all those prima donnas in the Senate. On the House side, the Appropriations Committee is the salt mine of the Congress. But senators are interested in flashy issues like foreign policy and the House has to do the grub work on appropriations.

Another member of the House committee saw the senators as dominated by minority groups and liberal influences. To him, it was the duty of the House to defend the nation against these minorities.

On the Senate side, the feelings of bitterness were no less intense. The House committee appeared to senators to be irresponsible and demagogic. A conservative senator summed up the case against the House:

> It's simple. The House members run every two years, and they've got to run as budget-cutters. Take subsidies for local airlines, for example. Under law, we've contracted to pay the airlines a certain amount. We can't avoid this. Yet we had the House cut this amount tremendously last year. This makes the House members look real good—"Look what *I'm* doing." The Senate has to close the gap on the absolutely necessary projects. It is truly amazing how the House clothes itself in a mantle of economy.

Toward the Minimization of Conflict

For the executive branch, the conflict has been a continuing headache. In 1963, House–Senate animosity flared up again and was an important element in a six-months appropriations lag which made planning extremely difficult for federal agencies. Because of the administrative complications which follow interhouse feuds, it is not surprising that reforms have been suggested which would minimize conflict in the appropriations process. In Chapter 6, we will attempt to analyze some of these reform proposals. But first we must see how congressional appropriations fit into the budgetary process as a whole.

2

THE BUDGETARY PROCESS

Although it is evident that the appropriations committees play a crucial part in the budgetary process, a description of the entire budgetary system is necessary for an understanding of the disruptions which intercommittee conflict can cause. And such a description must begin with the role of the President. For it is the Chief Executive who must make the highly political decisions involved in the early budgetary planning: where to cut or increase agency funds, whether to run a surplus or a deficit.

These questions involve economic considerations, and the President has special advisers in that field to aid him in his decision. Under the leadership of Dr. Walter Heller, the Council of Economic Advisers gained the attention of the nation during the administration of President John F. Kennedy. But the CEA is not the only source of economic advice open to the President; economists from the Bureau of the Budget and the Treasury Department participate in forecasting levels of federal revenue and expenditure. (All of this forecasting must be done for the year beginning two Julys in the future.) Although some attempt is made to keep revenues and expenditures in a close relationship with each other, a deficit budget may be used to stimulate a lagging economy—which will later increase government revenue.[1]

In order to forecast federal expenditures, it is necessary to predict agency needs for the coming fiscal years. The Bureau of the Budget (hereafter BOB) collects estimates which agencies have made in the past for the fiscal year under study, and certain important agencies are asked to review these estimates with representatives of the BOB. Then the President and the BOB Director study the budget together and the President outlines certain broad policy guidelines. Following this discussion, the BOB Director informs the heads of federal bureaus and departments of the President's decisions on the size of the budget and the ways in which funds are to be allocated.

Now the major scene of activity shifts to the government agency or bureau. The presidential recommendation, or "ceiling," is open to appeal from agencies and merely serves as a focus for bargaining. Having received the BOB's letter containing presidential guidelines, bureau chiefs call for estimates from their various subdivisions and offices. Estimates from these lower divisions are assembled carefully at the bureau level and passed on to a departmental budget committee. This committee has a difficult task, for it must reconcile bureau budgetary requests with departmental policy, with presidential guidelines, and with the expressed views of the mighty appropriations committees.

Once again, presidential control is asserted as the departmental requests are resubmitted to the BOB. Budget Bureau specialists hold both formal and informal meetings with departmental representatives, who present arguments in de-

1. For a discussion of the political and economic considerations underlying the President's budgetary decisions, see Nelson W. Polsby, *Congress and the Presidency* (Englewood Cliffs, Prentice-Hall, 1964). Chapter 6, on the budgetary process, provides a good bird's-eye view of budgeting and was extremely helpful in preparing this chapter.

fense of their requests. When these meetings are finished, the BOB assembles a final report for the President, who can make any adjustments that he feels are necessary. Letters are then sent to agencies informing them of the requests which the President will press in their behalf on Capitol Hill.

In late December, while the budget is being readied for the legislative onslaught, the Economic Report of the President and the State of the Union Message are being prepared. These two documents will explain the economic, political, and social considerations upon which the budget is based. In early January, all three documents are delivered to Congress by the President. The planning process is over, and the appropriations process is about to begin.

By tradition, the budget goes first to the House. It is referred to the Committee on Appropriations and split into twelve parts, along agency lines. Then it is given to subcommittees handling particular agencies' appropriations. Hearings are often lengthy, and they have been criticized for duplication and superficiality. Arthur W. Macmahon has said:

> The usefulness of the printed hearings is real but limited. Their great but largely unexplored value for the study of administration is another thing; these records are one of the main outcroppings of administrative methods. Some committee members say privately that the appropriations hearings are "junk." They doubt both whether the mass can be read and whether, if read, it enlightens the legislator. At the time a bill is being finally rewritten in the House committee, moreover, the printed hearings are not easy to use, for the index is not ready.[2]

2. Arthur W. Macmahon, "Congressional Oversight of Administration: The Power of the Purse," *Political Science Quarterly*, 57 (1943), 381.

From the executive branch, agency heads come to defend their requests, and for a government official such trips can be singularly unpleasant. Congressman Otto Passman's verbal attacks on foreign aid officials are well known, as are John Rooney's grillings of State Department men. Far from accepting a bureau's justifications of its own program, the appropriations committees may make funds available only on the condition that certain practices are changed or discontinued in the future. (This process will be explained later —see pp. 18–19.) The subcommittees may not appropriate money where there is no authorization, but they may refuse to appropriate money authorized by law.

After the hearings, each subcommittee meets in a "markup" session to hammer out a bill. Then the full House Committee on Appropriations usually adopts the subcommittee recommendations without changes. The next step is House passage, which is generally achieved easily. When an appropriations measure is ready, the Chairman negotiates for floor time directly with the Speaker and majority leader. There is no need for Rules Committee action; the Appropriations Committee has privileged access to the floor.[3]

The bill then goes to the Senate, where the sledding is much less hazardous. Senators do not go into the bills as deeply as do House members; rather, the occupants of the upper chamber focus their attention on cuts made by the House. In Senate hearings, agency representatives may complain about House cuts which they consider unfair, and often the Senate gives agencies the increases they desire.

When there are differences between the Senate and House bills—and this is often the case—the measure goes to conference. There a compromise is sought between the two versions of the appropriations measure. Following agree-

3. Polsby, p. 95.

ment on a compromise bill, the result goes back to each house for a final vote. As Nelson Polsby points out, the Senate and House conferees have a unique responsibility in the appropriations process:

> Because appropriations are necessary for the very running of the Government, the likelihood that such bills will be rejected by the House or Senate at the last stage or vetoed by the President is remote; this reposes an extra measure of responsibility and power upon members of appropriations conferences.[4]

In a later chapter, the conference will be examined more closely as a vital part of the appropriations process and as a locus of conflict within it.

THE EXECUTIVE–LEGISLATIVE RELATIONSHIP: POINTS OF CONTACT

In discussing the executive, planning segment of the budgetary process and the legislative, appropriating segment, it must not be assumed that there is a lack of communication between the two branches of government. For the appropriations committees have a profound effect on the early budgetary planning of agencies, and the agencies in turn are anxious to communicate with the committees about favorite projects. Further, there is communication—both antagonistic and cooperative—between the appropriations committees and the Bureau of the Budget.

One important method of communication is personal contact between appropriations committee (or staff) members and executive branch officials. In 1943 an observer noted:

> What is impressive, in tendency if not as matured fact, is the extent to which administrators meet with appro-

4. Ibid., p. 96.

priations subcommittees in *ad hoc* sessions during the year. Sometimes the administrators themselves seek the contact as a safeguard; sometimes they are summoned for admonition or worse. The subcommittees vary in the degree to which they engage in such activity. Much depends upon the chairman. But, generally speaking, interim supervisory relationships are increasing.[5]

The 1964 interviews suggested that close executive–legislative relationships continued to exist.

Another instance of personal contact occurs when administration officials petition the Senate Appropriations Committee to restore cuts made by the House. If the Senate committee is to fulfill its function as a court of appeals for the agencies, such communication is vital. In the summer of 1964, the Treasury Department requested the money to mint silver dollars. The House subcommittee handling Treasury appropriations denied the department the necessary funds. At this point, according to a Senate staff member, the following action ensued:

> The Treasury Department has a budget officer named ————. And our committee has a clerk by the name of ————. Treasury appealed to our committee to put $200,000 in the Treasury appropriations bill, and the clerk and budget officer went to work. They got together, set up a hearing and scheduled witnesses. Now, Dillon will come up to testify. The subcommittee will make a decision and recommend action by the full committee.

Thus, personal contacts help to bridge the legislative–executive gap in the appropriations process.

5. Macmahon, pp. 406–07.

Another communication channel is the reports of the committees on appropriations. Through the reports accompanying bills, the committees can tell bureau chiefs and department heads of the legislators' views on policy matters. The report, which is the work of the subcommittee, runs from 25 to 50 pages, including tables. In drafting a report, the subcommittee will sometimes consult departmental officers involved. If a departmental budget officer and a committee clerk shape a report together, then the resulting document is likely to contain remarks that may serve as tools by which the department can exercise leverage on its constituent bureaus.[6]

As a legal point, what is said in the report does not enter into the law that must be followed by the Treasury and the General Accounting Office. But the reports of an appropriations committee may be disregarded only at the risk of a cut in funds the following year. An illustration of the importance of committee reports is found in an incident concerning an appropriation for the National Labor Relations Board. In 1940, the Board's Division of Economic Research was under attack. Although the head of this unit was a highly controversial figure, the House appropriations subcommittee attack purported not to be personal. Rather, it was argued that the law did not authorize the NLRB to engage in "research." At any rate, the appropriation for the Board in fiscal 1941 was reduced by $337,000, and the report carried the suggestion that the Division of Economic Research be eliminated. The Division was eliminated, but most of its personnel were transferred to a new unit called the Division of Technical Service. Angered by the partial disregard of its report, the committee reduced the Board's appropriation by another $46,000. This time, the *bill* specifically denied salaries

6. Ibid., p. 388.

18

to members of the Division of Economic Research and the Division of Technical Service.[7]

For the appropriations committees, a final point of contact with the executive branch lies in their relations with the Bureau of the Budget. Sometimes the committees will criticize the BOB during agency hearings. The congressmen often pose leading questions to agency officials in an effort to determine the adequacy of BOB figures:

> *Official:* If I go into those questions my personal opinions might conflict with the Budget Report . . . But I want to make it clear to the committee that I have acquiesced in the limiting figure of the Budget.
> *Congressman:* You want this committee not to increase the amount of this Budget?
> *Official:* Oh, no; I recognize in Congress the power to do what it wants with this Budget.
> *Congressman:* Do you feel that it [library service] is adequate? . . .
> *Official:* It is all I am permitted to come here and ask you for.
> *Congressman:* How much would you like to ask for?
> *Official:* Oh, fifty percent more.[8]

In another instance, a subcommittee's warnings to BOB were explicit and forceful. The subcommittee on agricultural appropriations in the House reported in 1943 that it "has noticed, from time to time, the reluctance of bureau chiefs to answer inquiries propounded by its members respecting the adequacy of amounts granted by the Budget . . . and the wisdom, in the light of the public interest as they see it, of Budget reductions in such amounts."[9] Therefore, the

7. Ibid., pp. 391–94.
8. Polsby, p. 90.
9. Macmahon, pp. 408–09.

subcommittee asked agency men about the BOB's methods. What was the background of BOB men? Were they experts in agriculture? How long did they examine this part of the budget? The questioning ended with sharp minority criticism of the "captious and capricious" Budget Bureau and a threat to call BOB agricultural experts as witnesses before the committee.

This congressional sniping at BOB is one form of communication between the committees and the executive, but there is also a fair amount of legislative cooperation with the Budget Bureau. Especially fruitful collaboration has been carried out at times when a committee is made aware of a problem common to many of its appropriations bills. Then it may request BOB to report on the problem. In 1939, for example, the question of a general policy on administrative promotions was answered in this way. BOB made a study which became the basis of a statute, reflected in subsequent appropriations acts.[10] Also, there have been informal contacts between Budget Bureau staffs and the committees on appropriations.

Thus, a true understanding of the budgetary system requires something more than a study of the bare institutional mechanics of the process. For the executive and legislative participants do not face each other as two closed groups. Richard E. Neustadt has observed that our political system is one of "separated institutions *sharing* powers."[11] In this case, the sharing of budgetary powers between Congress and the Executive is facilitated by constant communication and contact between the two branches. Through personal contacts, agencies whose funds are cut by the House Appropriations Committee can carry their appeals to the Senate.

10. Ibid., pp. 412–13.
11. Richard E. Neustadt, *Presidential Power* (New York, John Wiley & Sons, 1960), p. 33.

Through committee reports, legislators can both influence agencies' budgetary requests and (by inviting government men to help in the writing of reports) draw agency representatives into the legislative budgetary process. Finally, by discussions at hearings and by seeking expert advice, the subcommittees have been brought into direct contact with the Bureau of the Budget. The chasm separating the executive from the legislative branch is crossed in the budgetary process by a variety of lines of communication. And this is an important point to make here, for we shall want to examine the effects of House–Senate feuding on these lines of communication and the ways in which they are used.

A MODEL OF PROBLEM-SOLVING

In his First Inaugural Address, Woodrow Wilson declared: "We shall deal with our economic system as it is and as it might be modified, not as it might be if we had a clean sheet of paper to write upon, and step by step we shall make it what it should be."[12] Writing in 1963, David Braybrooke and Charles E. Lindblom argued that "step by step" modification is the means by which problems are solved in our political system. They attacked a model of problem-solving often put forward by reformers, according to which the ideal way to make policy is to choose among alternatives after careful and complete study of all possible courses of action and all their possible consequences and after an evaluation of those results in the light of one's own value system. In other words, the policy problem is seen by some as an intellectual one; the planner must outline a program on the "clean sheet" mentioned by Wilson.

12. Quoted in David Braybrooke and Charles E. Lindblom, *A Strategy of Decision: Policy Evaluation as a Social Process* (New York, Free Press of Glencoe, 1963), pp. 26–27.

For Braybrooke and Lindblom, such a model of ideal policy-making is not applicable to the real world. Its advocates do not ordinarily use even a hypothetical example in expounding it, and the authors cannot cite a single historical example of its employment in policy analysis. To study seriously every alternative and every consequence of these alternatives in policy, it would be necessary "to list multitudes of possible links in multitudes of possible chains, with the phrase 'and so forth' endlessly repeated."[13] This exhaustive list of alternative policies provides no tactics or strategy for tackling problems in the world as we know it. Especially in the highly fluid realm of public affairs, say Braybrooke and Lindblom, the ideal model of decision-making is not applicable. A problem of reconciliation of interests is not a stable, well-formed problem that retains its outlines so firmly that all alternatives can be studied.

How, then, are decisions made in the political realm? The answer given is: through small or incremental moves on particular problems rather than through a comprehensive reform program. This process is really endless; it takes the form of an indefinite sequence of policy moves. Also, it is tentative and exploratory in that the goals of policy-making continue to change as fresh experience with policy throws new light on what is possible. (This is really moving *away* from known social ills rather than *toward* a known goal.)

For a democracy like the United States, the commitment to incremental change is not surprising:

> Nonincremental alternatives usually do not lie within the range of choice possible in the society or body politic. Societies . . . are complex structures that can avoid dissolution or intolerable dislocation only by meeting certain preconditions, among them that certain

13. Ibid., p. 41.

kinds of change are admissible only if they occur slowly. Political democracy is often greatly endangered by non-incremental change, which it can accommodate only in certain limited circumstances.[14]

In making decisions, policy analysts seek to improve their idea of present conditions and policies by obtaining more information about them. According to Lindblom's description of problem-solving, these analysts often gain information by comparing alternatives—all of which are similar to the status quo.

A policy analyst need not attempt to comprehend strictly and literally all present alternatives and future consequences of policy. Rather, he need only understand the respects in which various possible states differ from each other and from the status quo. Thus, Braybrooke and Lindblom describe decision-making as a process involving incremental moves on particular problems—an endless sequence of policy choices. We must now see whether this model helps to explain how decisions are made in the appropriations process.

THE STRATEGY OF BUDGETARY DECISIONS

James D. Barber of Yale University has conducted a valuable series of small-group experiments which bear on the problem of budgetary decision-making.[15] Barber arranged for thirteen Connecticut Boards of Finance to meet under controlled conditions and to solve a pair of hypothetical problems dealing with allocating a reduction in their most recent set of budgetary recommendations.

Barber found that the Boards sought to make their task easier by a number of characteristic ways of thinking. In the

14. Ibid., p. 73.
15. Described in James D. Barber, *Power in Committees* (Chicago, Rand McNally, 1966).

first place, a Board of Finance tended to remove from its consideration "terms over which it has little or no control." (Board members do not consider policy in a grand design; they work within the framework of facts with which they are most familiar.) Second, the Board repeatedly referred to the previous level and magnitude of expenditures: "the primary base-line for budget decision-making appears to be the last appropriation." Here again, the policy-maker does not try to comprehend all possible alternatives and consequences of policy. He merely attempts to understand the extent to which various possibilities differ from the status quo. In this way, notes Barber, certain categories are isolated for special attention. The predominant consideration is the effect of a cut on actual services rendered by the department; very seldom are expenditures in one department compared with those in another. Rather, the comparison is made with last year's figure for the same department. The process of decision-making is cautious—working with increments and focusing attention on the status quo.

Turning to the budgetary record of the federal government, it is possible to see that changes from year to year are marginal. Table 2.1 shows that the federal budget, as a percentage of GNP, has remained relatively constant.

TABLE 2.1. FEDERAL BUDGET AND GNP COMPARED

	1956	1957	1958	1959	1960	1961	1962	1963
Federal budget as a percentage of GNP	15.8	15.5	16.0	16.6	15.2	16.0	15.8	16.1

Source: Polsby, Congress and the Presidency, p. 86.

On the executive side of the budgetary system, decisions are not arrived at by a comparison of each program with every other program. Rather, the previous year's budget is used as a base from which to plan, and expected revenues are taken into account during the planning. Furthermore, the process of drawing up a departmental budget is not a completely scientific exercise. It must be partly political, for it is the result of bargaining between the President, the Budget Bureau, departmental officers, and bureau heads. Furthermore, agency budget officers must be careful not to antagonize important people on Capitol Hill. (In 1958, *Newsweek* quoted a State Department official as saying: "Let's face it. When Rooney whistles, we've just got to dance."[16]) Using the status quo as a base, executive branch officials move cautiously in adding politically acceptable segments to their budgetary requests.

An incremental model of decision-making seems equally applicable to the legislative side of the budgetary picture. Like executive administrators, congressmen do not often change their behavior radically from year to year. Table 2.2

TABLE 2.2. VARIATION IN ANNUAL APPROPRIATIONS

	Percentage change from previous year						
	0–5	6–10	11–20	31–40	41–50	51–100	101+
Cases (one agency per year = 1 case)	149	84	93	21	15	24	7
Total cases: 444							

Source: Wildavsky, *The Politics of the Budgetary Process,* p. 14.

indicates the marginal nature of changes in annual appropriations.

One powerful member of the Senate Appropriations Committee commented that "in doing appropriations, you just

16. *Newsweek,* April 7, 1958, p. 13.

don't worry about broad and explicit policy issues. Politics is dealing with people, and you can't make that exact." The comments of an insider in the appropriations process are valuable, but now further questions must be asked: In what specific ways does an incremental method of problem-solving manifest itself in the congressional appropriations process? What strategies do legislators pursue in attacking the budgetary problems they face?

In *The Politics of the Budgetary Process*, Aaron Wildavsky discusses certain of these strategies. For example, congressmen tend to specialize in their budgetary interests. The budget is not considered as a whole; rather, appropriations are broken up and considered piece-by-piece by numerous subcommittees. (Even within subcommittees, there are special subject areas.) Also, legislators take an historical approach to budgeting. Instead of focusing attention on various programs in their entirety, the committees usually concern themselves with the piecemeal development of those programs. The entire program is rarely subjected to annual scrutiny; congressmen concentrate instead on changes in various items—personnel, equipment, maintenance costs. To return to the Senate Appropriations Committee member, "it is seldom a question of policy . . . but policy can be expressed by cutting down the amounts."

Fragmentation is further increased by the Senate Appropriations Committee, which focuses its attention on items appealed from House decisions. The senators are therefore examining a small piece of the already reduced fragment considered by the House.

Finally, budgeting on Capitol Hill is sequential in nature. The appropriations committees do not even try to solve every problem at once; they do not deal with many problems in a given year and those they do take up are dealt with in different compartments. Over the years the subcommittees center now on one and then on another problem.

> When the budgetary decisions made by one subcommittee adversely affect those of another the difficulty is handled by "fire-truck tactics"; that is, by dealing with each problem in turn in whatever jurisdiction it appears. Difficulties are overcome not so much by central coordination or planning as by attacking each manifestation in the different centers of decision in sequence.[17]

Thus, the Braybrooke–Lindblom model for decision-making appears to be a useful guide in understanding the behavior of participants in the budgetary process. For budgeting can be usefully understood as an incremental process, proceeding from a continuing base. Decisions are fragmented and are made in response to conditions which are continually changing. Bureaucrats and congressmen rarely consider policy questions in their entirety and certainly do not evaluate each alternative and consequence of a policy move. Rather, they take limited steps toward solving particular problems.

Only by describing various methods of budgetary problem-solving can we consider the appropriations conference as an instrument for aiding legislators in their budgetary calculations. Furthermore, only by gaining an understanding of the budgetary system as a whole can we examine the functions (and dysfunctions) of intercommittee appropriations conflict for the entire system. Now we can concentrate on our twin star actors: the House and Senate Appropriations Committees.

17. Aaron B. Wildavsky, *The Politics of the Budgetary Process* (Boston, Little, Brown, 1964), p. 61.

3

FOCUS ON THE COMBATANTS:
THE APPROPRIATIONS COMMITTEES

What ... are some of the agencies of Congress which most directly affect the economy, which do or can serve to give a measure of coherence to economic legislation? Here selection is imperative; every committee of Congress has some impact. But the appropriations committees surely must be considered. Not only does the level of federal spending have direct and enormous influence on economic activity, but every piece of legislation which requires spending, and nearly every activity which wants to go on, must pass in review before these committees.[1]

The power and importance of the House and Senate Appropriations Committees have long been recognized by students of politics. And there is evidence that observers outside the social science community are becoming aware of the crucial nature of the appropriations committees' work. A recent article in *Science* magazine notes that, as football experts watch the movement of the line to understand each play, so may students of Congress focus their sights on the appropriations committees.[2] For in these committees, vital

1. Ralph K. Huitt, "Congressional Organization and Operations in the Field of Money and Credit," in Commission on Money and Credit, *Fiscal and Debt Management Policies* (Englewood Cliffs, Prentice-Hall, 1964), pp. 403–04.

2. *Science, 143* (February 7, 1964), 548–51.

decisions are being made: where to spend money, where to cut back, which government programs to encourage, and which programs to strangle by cutting off funds. It is to the House and Senate Appropriations Committees themselves that this study now turns. Without an understanding of the structure and operations of each committee, it is impossible to see the causes for conflict between the two and the preconditions necessary for reform in the budgetary process.

Surprising as it may seem to those who have confronted the entrenched and powerful appropriations committees, the clear-cut jurisdiction of these committees over all spending bills is just 45 years old. The Ways and Means Committee was established by the House of Representatives in 1802 with responsibility for both taxing and spending. A separate Committee on Public Expenditure was created twelve years later, but five additional committees were set up in 1816 to review the decisions of this committee.

In 1865 the House formed an Appropriations Committee; in 1867 the Senate followed suit. Once again, however, jurisdiction was split up over the years among several additional committees. Actually, unity of control came as a response to the Budgeting and Accounting Act of 1921. The legislature was now faced by a genuine budget from the executive side. As a reaction, Congress placed all spending power in its appropriations committees.[3]

THE HOUSE APPROPRIATIONS COMMITTEE: WIELDER OF POWER

Throughout the years, as has been noted, custom has conceded to the House the right to initiate appropriations bills. The House committee is larger than that of the Senate and

3. Huitt, p. 429.

its members can devote more time to appropriations business than can the senators (who must serve on other committees as well). Therefore, the House committee has historically played a larger role in the appropriations process. Furthermore, the chief obstacles to budgetary reform are to be found in the House Appropriations Committee. For these reasons, the discussion of the House committee will be more detailed than that of its counterpart in the upper house.

In a study of the House Appropriations Committee,[4] Richard F. Fenno gives evidence which clearly points up the fact of House committee power. Of 443 separate case histories of bureau appropriations examined, the House accepted Committee recommendations in 387 (or 87.4 per cent) of them. In 159 (33.6 per cent) of the cases studied, the House committee's original recommendations on money amounts were enacted into law without change.[5]

The words of a former congressman offer further testimony to the power of the Appropriations Committee. Discussing the "ways to get things done in Congress," the late Representative Clem Miller remarked:

> To tackle the Appropriations Committee on the Floor of the House is a major decision, frequently the most important decision a Member will make that term of Congress. Here is the choice. If he is silent, perhaps the Senate will restore the item to the bill. If he speaks up and is beaten, he will *never* get it back. And the chances of winning are better than five hundred to one against. These odds mean silence to most congressmen.[6]

4. Richard F. Fenno, Jr., "The House Appropriations Committee as a Political System: The Problem of Integration," *American Political Science Review*, 56 (1962), 310–24.

5. Ibid., p. 323.

6. Clem Miller, *Member of the House: Letters of a Congressman* (New York, Charles Scribner's Sons, 1962), pp. 39–40.

Nowhere is the committee's power more acutely felt or more bitterly resented than in the field of foreign policy. In theory, the Appropriations Committee merely determines whether all of the dollars requested to carry out what Congress has authorized are really needed. The money committees do not, it is supposed, alter the substance of policies. Of course, practice does not always conform to theory. Holbert N. Carroll, viewing the Appropriations Committee warily, pointed out that

> the Committee on Appropriations . . . is the most powerful agency of control over the course of policies and their administration in the House of Representatives. Almost all important foreign policies require money for support, so in deciding what funds shall be allowed, and in sundry other ways . . . the committee wields great influence over the substance of policies. Since the decisions of this committee follow in the wake of formal policy decisions, its word is the last word, so far as the House is concerned, respecting these policies.[7]

The committee exercises its power in a variety of ways. First and foremost among its weapons is the power to cut off an agency's funds. In three areas studied by Professor Carroll (occupation funds 1946–51, foreign aid 1947–56, and State Department budgets 1945–56), the executive branch submitted estimates totaling $54.8 billion. The committee reported 88.7 per cent of the funds requested by the executive, and the voice of the committee was the voice of the House. In thirty out of thirty-five major appropriations, the House simply endorsed the committee's bill.[8] To demonstrate its disagreement with the large-scale European recovery pro-

7. Holbert N. Carroll, *The House of Representatives and Foreign Affairs* (Pittsburgh, University of Pittsburgh Press, 1958), pp. 141–42.
8. Ibid., p. 154.

gram, the committee slashed more than one billion dollars from the Marshall Plan's funds.

In Chapter 2, it was shown that committee *reports* can often be used to exercise control over executive branch activities. Another weapon of the committee is the insertion of limitations and legislative provisions in bills themselves. The rules of the House forbid legislation in appropriations bills, but limitations which specify that no part or only a fraction of an appropriation may be used for a certain purpose are quite in order. And sometimes limitations of a distinctly legislative nature slip through the House unchallenged. Thus, in providing funds for aid in occupied countries in 1947, the committee added a provision that the countries to receive aid "shall be expected to provide, in agreements to be signed by their governments . . . for reimbursement to the United States for such aid."[9] The Appropriations Committee had initiated a major policy innovation.

"Standing Like a Stone Wall": *The Self-Integration of the House Committee*

In an exchange with a member of the House Appropriations Committee, Representative Clarence Brown remarked bitterly that when an amendment is offered

> to reduce an appropriations item, the Appropriations Committee stands like a stone wall most of the time, saying "no, you mustn't touch this." That is one of the things that has brought complaint against your committee, sir, and you know it . . .[10]

The committee does seem to stand like a "stone wall." In contrast to the House Committee on Education and Labor, where lack of internal unity resulted in the inability of that

9. Ibid., p. 168.
10. Wildavsky, *The Politics of the Budgetary Process*, p. 50.

committee to propose a successful federal aid to education bill during the Eisenhower and Kennedy Administrations,[11] the House Appropriations Committee is remarkably well integrated. Fenno suggests that this tight integration is in large measure responsible for the power and legislative success of the committee.[12] In 1964 most of the congressmen and staff members interviewed mentioned the high degree of cohesion found in the House committee and some attempted to give explanations for it. Because committee integration may have some effect on House strength in conference situations and House committee resistance to reform, it is necessary to examine the reasons for it.

The need for integration in a given social system arises from the differentiation among its constituent elements. A committee must make these diverse parts work together in support of one another. Committee integration may be defined as the "degree to which there is a working together or a meshing together or mutual support among its roles and its subgroups."[13] A concomitant of tight integration is the existence of control mechanisms—rewards and penalties—which are capable of maintaining conformity to the norms.

Fenno's work on the House Appropriations Committee focuses on the period 1947–61. His analysis includes a listing of characteristics of the committee which help explain the integration of its parts and a description of the control mechanisms that preserve integration. The present study makes use of Fenno's outline and general explanation of committee integration, but the analysis here is based on in-

11. Richard F. Fenno, Jr., "The House of Representatives and Federal Aid to Education," in R. L. Peabody and N. W. Polsby, eds., *New Perspectives on the House of Representatives* (Chicago, Rand McNally, 1963), p. 352.

12. Fenno, "House Appropriations Committee," p. 323.

13. Ibid., p. 310.

terviews carried out in the Spring and Summer of 1964. Therefore, relevant examples and illustrations will be drawn from the more recent interview material. At certain points, Professor Fenno's analysis will be qualified.

First of all, Fenno sees integration aided by a well-articulated and deeply rooted consensus on committee goals and tasks. The committee's view is rooted in the traditional preeminence of the House in appropriations affairs. Moving from this, the committee sees itself as the most important unit in the appropriations process. For the committee, its most important task is guarding the Federal Treasury—usually by cutting down budget estimates. And the House committee does indeed cut estimates. For the purposes of a larger study, Fenno examined the case histories of appropriations for 37 executive bureaus over a twelve-year period: 1947–59. Of 443 separate bureau estimates, the committee reduced 77.2 per cent of them.

However, one must be careful of the generalization that House Appropriations Committee members are budget-cutters. The *Science* article referred to above also commended Representative John E. Fogarty (D., R.I.) for his knowledge of scientific and medical affairs. As chairman of the subcommittee on Labor-Health, Education and Welfare Appropriations, Fogarty has consistently championed the cause of the National Institutes of Health. Further, there are members who identify with an agency or with specific programs. "To me, forestry has become a religion," once remarked Representative Walter Horan. And Daniel Flood has kept a protective eye on Defense Department appropriations.[14] Thus, Fenno's identification of committee consensus may be qualified to say that budget-cutting is not the *only* role which motivates Appropriations Committee members. The exceptions must be taken into account.

14. Wildavsky, p. 48.

Integration in the Appropriations Committee is also facilitated by the subject matter with which the group deals. Writing in 1943, Macmahon spoke of the traditional "appropriations type: hard-working, hard-bitten."[15] Fenno observes that a money decision does not seem to be a vital policy decision; thus members are relatively free of "liberal" and "conservative" roles inside the committee. "The Appropriations Committee is the banker for the federal government," drawled one southern House committee member in 1964. "Appropriations bills are more or less dull. They all concern dollars and cents. Nothing we do is really earth-shaking—we finance programs, that's all." Integration appears to be further facilitated by the fact that a man recruited for the Appropriations Committee is first informally certified as a "responsible legislator"—defined as "one whose ability, attitudes and relationships with his colleagues serve to enhance the prestige and importance of the House of Representatives."[16] Such a man has a basic respect for the legislative process and appreciates its informal rules. This quality is the most important criterion for assignment to the three top House committees—Rules, Ways and Means, and Appropriations. In the interviews, the friendly southern congressman commented that "the members of this committee are picked carefully—believe me." Only "responsible legislators"—those who are willing to compromise and who are dedicated to the ways of the House of Representatives—need apply.

Another factor in the committee's integration is the attractiveness of the Appropriations Committee for its members. This strong attraction increases the influence which the committee and its norms exercise on all members, for "it

15. Macmahon, "Congressional Oversight of Administration," p. 177.
16. Nicholas A. Masters, "Committee Assignments," in Peabody and Polsby, p. 46.

increases the susceptibility of the newcomer to Committee socialization and of the veteran to Committee sanctions applicable against deviant behavior."[17]

Note has already been made of the "appropriations type" —hard-working and industrious. Consider the following statistics:

> The House was in session 141 days during the first session of the Eighty-sixth Congress. In that period the Defense Subcommittee of the Appropriations Committee . . . met sixty-five days, nearly always in both morning and afternoon sessions. For nearly three and one-half months the subcommittee met almost daily on the dual meeting basis. In 1963, the Defense Subcommittee met seventy two and one-half working days, excluding the period required for marking up the Defense Appropriations bill.[18]

Committee members revel in their role of hard-working legislators. "We try to build up respect for each other on the committee. We think we're the hardest working committee in Congress," remarked a conservative member of the committee. Observed a young liberal: "I may sound critical, but a lot of hard work is done by those subcommittees . . . They are very conscientious. No glory, no public hearings . . . this is a working committee."

These characteristics of the House Appropriations Committee—consensus, careful recruitment, nature of the work, and committee attractiveness—help to explain the integration of the committee. But how is integration maintained? By what mechanisms are decisions made?

17. Fenno, "House Appropriations Committee," p. 314.

18. Charles L. Clapp, *The Congressman: His Work as He Sees It* (Garden City, N.Y., Doubleday Anchor Books, 1963), p. 267.

The committee carries on its day-to-day work in subcommittees, each of which is given jurisdiction over a number of related governmental units. The chairman of the full committee sets the number and jurisdiction of subcommittees and appoints their chairmen and majority party members, while the ranking minority member decides which minority members shall be included. Each subcommittee holds hearings on its agencies' budgets, writes the full committee's report on those agencies' appropriations, and handles the debate on the floor. And each subcommittee, within its jurisdiction, is proudly independent. "Subcommittee chairmen are kings unto themselves," said one Republican member. Another member—this one a Democrat—remarked that:

> Rather than a committee, this is a collection of thirteen principalities. When we have a meeting of the full committee, it is perfunctory and almost pro forma. Although the issues are thoroughly gone into in subcommittee, you have no chance to do so in full committee. Try to get reports in advance, and you find that it is a tightly guarded secret.

In order to make this policy of subcommittee autonomy work, a norm of specialization exists. Each member is expected to play the role of specialist in the activities of one subcommittee. Conflict among subcommittees is reduced by the deference traditionally accorded to the recommendation of the subcommittee which has "the facts." An older committee member observed: "There is great specialization. And look at the *esprit de corps* in the committee." Furthermore, integration is facilitated by the norm of subcommittee unity, a willingness to support the recommendations of one's own subcommittee. (If the norm of reciprocity—the custom which requires that each subcommittee respect the work done with-

37

in every other specialized unit—functions to minimize conflict in the full committee, then the norm of unity minimizes conflict within the subcommittee.) There is a tradition against minority reports in both the subcommittee and the full committee. During the period 1947–57, for example, only 9 out of a possible 141 were written. Also, there is a tradition of nonpartisanship within both the subcommittees and full committee. The committee has a nonpartisan staff; requests for studies by the committee's investigating staff must be made by the chairman and ranking member of the full committee and also the chairman and ranking member of the subcommittee involved. With party conflict minimized, integration is facilitated. "Partisan loyalty fades almost entirely," remarks one member, while another adds: "There are no Republican–Democrat battles. This is just not natural —it's phenomenal!"[19]

One source of internal cohesion and integration is the effective control mechanism of socialization and sanction. Members must learn to see the world around them with some degree of similarity. A liberal member of the committee has remarked:

> The Appropriations Committee develops a strange sort of breed. As soon as you get on the committee, somehow you become more responsible as a member of Congress. You find you have to justify expenditures and you can-

19. One exception to the rule of nonpartisanship was the creation, in the 88th Congress, of the "Bow" task force of House Republican members of the committee. This group worked in cooperation with the minority leadership to cut the President's budget. One member, Rep. Pillion, observed "For the first time in my memory, the Republican members of the Appropriations Subcommittees worked as a team with specific appropriation reduction targets." See John S. Saloma, III, *The Responsible Use of Power: A Critical Analysis of the Congressional Budget Process* (Washington, American Enterprise Institute, 1964), p. 33.

not pass over any situation very lightly. As a result you become more conservative.[20]

Socialization is carried out by a system of rewards and punishments. For the member who serves his apprenticeship on the committee, who follows the norms of subcommittee autonomy and unity, who does not express dissent on the floor, there are rewards—perhaps prominent floor roles, perhaps a subcommittee chairmanship.

For those who insist on breaking committee norms, there are punishments. One liberal had this to say:

> We had an appropriation in the Interior bill for the Kennedy Cultural Center. In subcommittee, we discussed it—and I thought the subcommittee decided on a ridiculous location. I said so on the floor. Boy, was my subcommittee chairman furious! He gave me a tremendous tongue-lashing.

Another remarked:

> On the foreign aid appropriation, I filed dissenting remarks with the clerk. They didn't print them, and the chairman told me that they wouldn't print minority opinions unless they came from that subcommittee's members. Believe me, I've gotten into a lot of trouble for sounding off like this . . .

In the 1964 interviews, liberals who criticized committee procedures justified their willingness to "go along" by declaring their great admiration for the work of their subcommittee chairmen. Thus, a northern Democrat remarked: "Al Thomas and Rooney are good men . . . really great. And Rooney knows what he's doing . . . he talks tough but his bark is worse than his bite." Thus, we may add another factor

20. Clapp, p. 243.

promoting committee integration: respect for the men who lead the subcommittees.

Fenno's emphasis on subcommittee unity and autonomy may be modified slightly. At times, intervention by the chairman of the full committee may be necessary to curb actions by a subcommittee chairman which block party programs deemed vital. Thus, in the summer of 1964, Representative George H. Mahon, new chairman of the Appropriations Committee, lobbied actively to save President Johnson's foreign aid bill from its annual emasculation at the hands of Representative Otto Passman (D., La.) in the Foreign Operations subcommittee.

Still, Fenno's analysis seems to be borne out by interview material collected in 1964. The consensus, attractiveness, and recruitment policies of the Committee on Appropriations make it susceptible to tight integration. Decisions are made in specialized subcommittees, and dissent and partisanship are discouraged. Each subcommittee respects the work of the others, and all members stand together on the floor. Finally, to encourage compliance with the set of norms (i.e. informal but authoritative rules for behavior), a system of rewards and punishments is maintained. All of this keeps the House Appropriations Committee functioning as a cohesive and well-integrated unit. Potentially divisive subgroups—conservatives and liberals, rural and urban men, Republicans and Democrats—are brought together and mesh to form a well-functioning whole. Conflict is minimized, and work can go on effectively.

The Role of the Chairman

Although the appropriations subcommittees are fairly autonomous, the power of the chairman of the full committee cannot be denied. For it is he who selects the subcommittee chairmen and the majority members of each sub-committee. Clarence Cannon, who was chairman of the committee until the spring of 1964, put his unique stamp on the House Appropriations Committee.

> In 1956 he [Cannon] reorganized the subcommittees, in the course of which he deprived Rep. Vaughn Gary, who was perhaps not sufficiently staunch in his opposition to the foreign aid program, of the chairmanship of the relevant subcommittee . . . [and he] would have gone further, were he not restrained by the protests of his senior colleagues on the Committee . . . In 1962 he reached into the budget for the Defense Department . . . plucked out the Civil Defense program . . . and assigned it to a subcommittee whose chairman opposed the program. In 1963 five liberal new members were placed on the Committee by the leadership, replacing, on the average, more conservative men. Cannon gave all but one of the new members low-level jobs in the Committee's equivalent of Siberia: subcommittees on the District of Columbia, on the legislative budget, and for a man from New York City, the subcommittee on agriculture. Meanwhile, senior members whose views were more congenial sat on three or four important subcommittees simultaneously.[21]

One senior member of the committee remarked that "Cannon is always there when they mark up a bill." Another explained that "the subcommittee chairmen are really kings of their own castles. But Cannon can be the swing vote on markups. On Public Works, Cannon can work with Republicans to kill a bill."

However, Clarence Cannon did not prove immortal—perhaps surprising some Washington observers. On May 12,

21. Polsby, *Congress and the Presidency,* pp. 91–92.

1964, he died of a heart ailment at the age of 85. The new chairman was George H. Mahon of Texas, and the *New York Times* was quick to evaluate the newcomer:

> Administration leaders do not expect any sudden change in the 50-member committee's conservative budget-cutting proclivities. Mr. Mahon, like his predecessor, is a conservative and an outspoken advocate of economy in government. However, it is generally accepted that the 63-year-old Texan will be much easier to work with than was the crusty, 85-year-old Mr. Cannon.[22]

Prophetically, the *Times* went on to note that "a possible by-product of the shift in chairmen is a gradual decline in the power of Otto E. Passman, Chairman of the Foreign Operations subcommittee." We have already indicated that this decline did indeed occur. Instead of supporting Mr. Passman, as Mr. Cannon had done, the new chairman used persuasion effectively to turn Passman's subcommittee against its chairman by a vote of 7–5 and thus to save the Administration's foreign aid package in 1964. The following winter, at the start of Congress, Chairman Mahon stacked Passman's subcommittee overwhelmingly against him. When the subcommittee voted a generous foreign aid bill in the summer of 1965 (trimmed by only $75 million), Representative Passman decided to serve as floor manager of the bill anyway. What followed was one of the weirdest performances in Congressional history:

> For 52 minutes, while he presented his own bill to the House, Passman savagely attacked it and all "the imaginary accomplishments of the foreign aid program." And then, after fulsome apologies, Passman turned around and started fighting for the bill. "I represent the ma-

22. *New York Times,* May 13, 1964.

jority of the committee and not necessarily my personal views," he said. "It will be my responsibility to defend it to the fullest extent of my ability." When Republicans moved to cut $285 million out of it, Passman declared: "I hope the motion will be voted down."[23]

As the *Times* had predicted, the area of foreign affairs was the scene of the major change in appropriations policy under the new chairman.

Interviews with two high-ranking House staff members confirmed the *Times'* assessment. One remarked: "There have been no significant changes in the House committee since Mahon took over. He is not the type to rush in. There will be differences, like in foreign aid. But basically Mr. Mahon is at least as conservative as Mr. Cannon." The other offered much the same analysis:

> Mahon is averse to using brutal power. But he realizes that he is the chairman. He is just as vigorous as Cannon, although less spectacular. And Mahon is as conservative as Cannon, but not as obvious about it. I mean he doesn't adopt a meat-axe approach and cut willy-nilly.

Neither the temperament of the chairman nor the solidarity of the committee encourages sweeping changes. And, although Mr. Mahon is not as pugnacious as his predecessor, much hostile feeling still exists between the House and Senate Appropriations Committees. For, as we have shown, hostility between the committees runs deeper than the personalities of committee chairmen. (Although Mr. Mahon might not be as active a catalyst of conflict as was Mr. Cannon, it must be remembered that a change in Senate committee leadership might make that group *more* pugnacious. So there are still possibilities of open battle in the future;

23. *Time,* September 17, 1965, p. 38.

as we shall see, legislators in 1965 worried about House–Senate feuds and tried to devise ways to deal with them.)

Still, Mr. Mahon *has* made a change in an appropriations subcommittee, and that change may be instructive for those who would make further alterations in the appropriations process. In 1964, the chairman was able to go over the head of a subcommittee chairman to ensure passage of a party measure in an election year. At that time, the power of the party over its members was strong enough to win out over subcommittee loyalties. Further, the change was incremental and came in stages. In 1964 Chairman Mahon used persuasion to change the votes of subcommittee members. In 1965 the chairman of the full committee reshuffled the membership of the Foreign Operations subcommittee to make it more "reasonable." These were incremental changes, particularly applicable to a budgetary process in which sweeping alterations are shunned.

The House Staff: Professionalism and Nonpartisanship

"We have a good appropriations staff. Nobody's political friend is on the staff. These people come from GAO—and Mr. Cannon keeps it that way—no political influence. You know, a competent staff is the right arm of this committee." With these words, a liberal member of the House committee paid tribute to a committee staff which is well known for its hard work and lack of partisanship.

Each subcommittee has access to professional staff assistance. Unlike most congressional committees, the Committee on Appropriations has had a history of employing professional help that reaches back into the 1920s; today, the committee conducts a modest training program to develop the competence of both senior and junior staff members.[24] The

24. Carroll, p. 148.

majority and minority each employs a small political staff which is separated from the bulk of the professional staff.

In numbers, the staff of the Appropriations Committee appears large. In the late 1950s the size of the staff averaged about sixty to seventy-five employees. (The numbers have remained remarkably stable from 1951 to the present day.) But these figures include stenographic and clerical help; only twenty could really be classified as professionals. There were also two or three investigators employed by the committee and a large number of special investigators borrowed from the executive branch for temporary duties (for the second half of 1955 there were thirty-four such investigators on the committee's staff).

Whether or not the staff of this committee is adequate to its task has been argued back and forth for years. In the interviews, Appropriations Committee members from both houses expressed the view that a larger professional staff was needed. However, the controversy over staff size is not a main concern of this study. Suffice it to say that the staff of the House Appropriations Committee, by its nonpartisan nature, reduces the chances for partisan conflict on the committee. Furthermore, the competence and unusual *esprit de corps* of the staff deepens the attraction which the committee has for its members and thus aids cohesion and integration.

THE SENATE COMMITTEE

Although the Senate Appropriations Committee is only half as large as its counterpart in the House (twenty-seven as opposed to fifty members, to be exact), and although it waits for the House to act before submitting its own report, the Senate committee is not weak. It is composed of senior and powerful men, like Richard B. Russell of Georgia, Warren G. Magnuson of Washington, Mike Mansfield of

Montana, and Thomas H. Kuchel of California. In the second session of the 84th Congress, the Appropriations Committee contained nine chairmen or ranking minority members of other committees, the Democratic floor leader and whip, the Republican floor leader, whip, and Policy Committee chairman.[25] Of the twenty-three men who made up the committee in the 85th Congress, five had been in the Senate more than twenty years, another twelve for ten years or more, and only one less than six years. Most had been members of the House of Representatives, seven for more than ten years. Among them, they represented 303 years of service in the Senate and 428 years in Congress.[26]

The Senate committee is obviously an attractive one. A senior member said: "The Appropriations Committee in any legislative body is at the top . . . In the Appropriations Committee, you find the greatest education in government. The spread of jurisdiction is tremendous." One indication of difference in committee attractiveness is the movement of senators from one committee to another. Because any change in committee assignment involves a loss of committee seniority, a change usually indicates that a senator prefers the new committee to the old. In an attempt to measure the relative attractiveness of committees, Donald R. Matthews constructed a chart showing the net effects of all changes in Senate committee assignments during the 1947–57 period (see Table 3.1). The extreme right-hand column shows the net gain or loss of each committee.

Based on this measure, the Committee on Appropriations is second only to Foreign Relations in attractiveness. One

25. Donald R. Matthews, *U.S. Senators and Their World* (New York, Vintage Books, 1960), p. 151.

26. Thomas E. Barth and Sandra Jo LeGath, *The Appropriations Process in the Senate* (unpublished M.A. thesis, University of Wisconsin, 1960).

TABLE 3.1. NET GAIN OR LOSS OF COMMITTEE MEMBERSHIP THROUGH CHANGE OF ASSIGNMENT, 80TH THROUGH 84TH CONGRESSES.

COMMITTEE	Foreign Relations	Appropriations	Finance	Armed Services	Agriculture	Judiciary	Commerce	Banking & Currency	Interior	Public Works	Labor	Government Operations	Rules	Post Office	D.C.	NET TOTALS
1. Foreign Relations		+2	+2	+1	+2	+1	+1	+1	+1	+1	+2	+3	+1	+1	+1	+16
2. Appropriations	−2		+1	+2	+1	+1	+1	+1	+1	+3	+1	+1	+1	+3	+1	+15
3. Finance	−2	−1		+1	+1		0	+2	+2	+2	+1		+2	+1	+2	+10
4. Armed Services	−1	−2	−1							+1		+3	+3		+1	+4
5. Agriculture	−2		−1				+1	+1		+1	+2	+2	+1	+1	+3	+7
6. Judiciary	−1	−1					+1			+2	0	+2	+1	+1	+1	+8
7. Interstate & Foreign Commerce	−1	−1						0	+2	+1		+2	+2	+4	+1	+8
8. Banking & Currency	−1	−1	0		−1		0		0	+1		+1	+3	0	−1	+1
9. Interior	−1			−2	−1		0	0			+1			+1		+2
10. Public Works	−1	−3	−2	−1	−1	−1	−2						+1	+4	+2	−5
11. Labor & Public Welfare	−2	−1	−2	−1	−1	−2	−1	−1	−1	−1		+2		+4	−1	−6
12. Government Operations	−3	−3	−1	−1	−3	−2	0	−2	−1	−1	−2		+1		+3	−11
13. Rules	−1	−1	−1	−3	−1	−1	−2	−3	−1	−1		−1		+1	+4	−9
14. Post Office	−1	−3	−1		−1	−1	−4	0	−1	−4		−1	−3		+1	−19
15. District of Columbia	−1	−1	−2	−1	−3	−1	−1	+1	−1	−2	+1	−3	−4	−1		−17

Source: Matthews, *U.S. Senators and Their World*, p. 149.

reason seems obvious: a member of the Appropriations Committee is in a position to "do more for his constituency" in terms of federal projects. (Thus, Senator Mansfield's position on the Appropriations Committee was crucial in the decision by that body to appropriate money for the minting of silver dollars in the summer of 1964. This decision, of course, helped the silver interests in Montana tremendously.) Furthermore, it is felt that an Appropriations Committee member can exert more influence in his dealings "downtown"—with the executive branch.

In 1962 the senators demanded that they be given the opportunity to initiate one half of all appropriations measures. But the interviews showed that members of the upper house felt pressed for time under their present duties. One senior member of the Senate committee observed: "In the Senate, too many people have to serve on too many committees. There is a *tremendous* amount of time required, and I have so much to do. I may have two to six meetings in the morning. Shall I divide my time among these? Or shall I specialize?" With Appropriations Committee members serving on (and sometimes chairing) other major committees, how could they possibly hope to initiate and hold lengthy hearings on half the appropriations bills? The senior committee member had this answer: "The Senate could initiate appropriations, but it would have to make time for this. We would have to spread ourselves less thin. In fact, I would say that the Appropriations Committee members should have no other committees." Perhaps the Senate's demand in 1962 for the right to initiate appropriations can best be understood as a demand to be used for bargaining purposes. At any rate, the Senate committee at the present time does perform a distinctive function in the appropriations process, and it is to that function that the study must now turn.

The Court of Appeals

The Senate has acted as an appeals agency. The House trims, and the agencies run with their tear-jerking story to the Senate. "We got 98% and we're going to wail and groan about the 2% that the House cut out." They pick out the things in which the Senate is the most interested.

Thus a House committee staff member described the appellate function of the Senate Appropriations Committee. A Senate subcommittee chairman remarked: "It would be an effort in futility for the Senate to go into each detail. In practice, the Senate has emphasized the effort to reverse House decisions."

In 12 of 21 appropriations for fiscal 1958 involving over half the total appropriations, the Senate restored all or part of the cuts made by the House.[27] Further evidence of the Senate's appellate function is found in the testimony of committee members. In 1957 Senator Magnuson, chairman of the Independent Offices subcommittee, sent letters to all heads of affected agencies asking if the "public interest" required any changes in the House appropriations bill and whether they wanted to arrange a hearing. Also, when Secretary of Commerce Weeks assumed that the Senate subcommittee would consider his whole budget (and not just the six items appealed by the department), Senator Holland set him straight: "The lack of appeal would indicate . . . that you think the other cuts except in the six items which you want to mention will not be so harmful as to require your making

27. Huitt, p. 434.

an appeal . . . In other words, we are not going to appeal for you."[28]

As Huitt notes, however, there is one potent restraint on appeals (and this restraint operates more effectively on service agencies like the Library of Congress than on agencies with strong and well-organized clienteles). That is the prospect of facing the members of the House committee the year after a successful appeal has been carried off. The next time, the cut might be deeper. For the House might count on the Senate's exercising its power to rescue the agency again.

In foreign affairs, the Senate committee exercises an appellate function in regard to both funds and policy directives. Of thirty-five major appropriations in the three foreign policy areas studied by Carroll, the Senate raised the House-approved sums in twenty-four. The executive branch submitted estimates calling for almost $55 billion for the thirty-five major appropriations. For all three areas combined, the Senate committee approved sums 6.7 per cent higher than House-endorsed sums. Senate sums were 14.9 per cent higher in the area of occupation, 6 per cent higher in foreign aid, and 3.5 per cent higher for the State Department.[29]

It is interesting to note that the appellate behavior of the Senate committee extends to substantive matters as well. Phrases are sometimes inserted in the reports of the Senate committee to permit administrators to evade some of the detailed and bothersome instructions contained in House reports. In 1948, when the House committee slashed Marshall Plan funds by about one fourth, the Senate committee restored a substantial portion of the money cut out by the House and also removed or changed legislative decisions

28. Ibid.
29. Carroll, p. 291.

sponsored by the House committee which diverged from decisions approved in the authorizing committees.

A Word on the Staff

The Senate committee has enjoyed marked continuity of staff, as has its counterpart in the lower chamber. Thomas P. Cleaves was clerk from 1873 to 1910 and Kenneth F. Rea served from 1910 to 1939. Everard H. Smith, the present clerk, took that position in 1939.[30] As in the House, Senate staff spirit runs high. One assistant remarked: "We get our talent from the executive branch, and they had better be trained in accounting. The pay is lower on the Hill, but it's worth it to be with this committee." Professional talent—including accountants and lawyers—is hired from the executive branch. Senate staffers are proud to be with the committee and recall with avid interest the House–Senate battle of 1962. House members are seen as "irresponsible," and special condemnation was reserved for Representative Otto Passman, the once terrifying villain of Foreign Operations conferences. In all, the competent Senate staff serves for its committee a function similar to that provided by the House staff for its superior body. The staff adds a further element of attractiveness and cohesion to the Senate Appropriations Committee. Of course, the staff's attitude toward the House does not encourage peaceful relations between the committees, and Senate staffers were quick to say—without regret—that House–Senate conflict could easily break out again.

Thus, at the center of the appropriations process, there are two proud and powerful committees. Filled by some of the most prominent men in Congress, the two groups have very different roles. The House committee, viewing itself as

30. Macmahon, p. 184.

the voice of economy, seeks to cut excess "fat" from the appropriations requests of various agencies. On the other hand, the Senate committee, perceiving itself as the defender of responsibility and continuity in government, serves as a court of appeals for agencies whose budget requests have been cut by the House. The House (in most cases) slashes funds; the Senate (in most cases) restores either part or all of the House cuts. Somehow, these forces must meet; the matter must be resolved. A figure must be settled upon which will be acceptable to both sides. Thus the matter moves to conference committee.

4

CONFERENCE

The House rejects the Senate's amendments without hearing them read, the Senate stoutly refuses to yield; a conference ensues . . . and a compromise is effected, by such a compounding of disagreeing propositions as gives neither party to the quarrel the victory . . . [Conference] reports are matters of the highest prerogative. They may be brought in even while a member is speaking. It is much better to silence a speaker than to delay for a single moment, at this stage of the session, the pressing, imperious question of the supplies for the support of the government . . . It is evident, therefore, that after all the careful and thoroughgoing debate . . . they [appropriations] finally pass in a very chaotic state, full of provisions which neither the House nor the Senate likes, and utterly vague and unintelligible to every one save the members of the Conference Committee . . .

Woodrow Wilson,
Congressional Government[1]

Today, as in Woodrow Wilson's time, the conference committees (special committees to resolve differences between House and Senate versions of a bill) play a crucial part in the appropriations process. The end of a congressional ses-

1. Woodrow Wilson, *Congressional Government* (New York, Meridian Books, 1956; 1st ed., 1884), pp. 114–15.

sion is characterized by the hurried discussion and passage of bills which contain funds to provide for "the support of the government." These bills are appropriations bills—and most of them are passed only after conference deliberation.

The examination of appropriations conferences between the two houses is extremely important for the purposes of this study. For the conference is the place of interaction between the two committees and the point at which conflict becomes apparent. In 1962 the appropriations war was sparked by a dispute over conference location and procedure; the conflict became so intense that conferences were discontinued altogether.

Even when representatives of the committees do meet in conference, hostility between the two is likely to arise. Remarking that "the interesting conferences are in foreign aid," one Senate staff member described the action which takes place in such conferences:

> It gets pretty rough and hot. They meet at ten, quit at twelve, go back at three and quit at five. This goes on for three or four days. Sometimes both sides would get up and walk out. These men are gentlemen, but there is strong feeling on both sides.

Later in the book, the roots—and consequences—of conflict will be examined. This chapter will be devoted to a study of the behavior of appropriations committee members in a specific conflict situation: the conference.

A number of approaches will be used to examine conference behavior. First, a general description of the mechanics of the conference will be given. Then, an analysis will be made of the various strategies used by bargaining "teams" in an appropriations conference. Finally, we shall see how the conference fits into the decision-making model discussed in Chapter 2. That model was left half-finished; now, it must be shown how conference committee battles serve a function in "incremental" budgeting.

The conference committee comes into being when disagreement is formally stated by one house of Congress or the other. Usually this happens when the second house has amended a bill and returned it to the house of origin, which refuses to accept the amendment. Not infrequently, however, the second house assumes that the house of origin will refuse to accept the change. In this case, the second house will vote to insist and will request a conference without ever returning the bill to the house of origin.[2] Appropriations bills often go to conference because the Senate advocates the expenditure of higher sums than does the House. But disagreements are also provoked by legislative directives attached by one house which are obnoxious to the other. For example, the Urgent Deficiency Appropriation of 1943 contained a House-sponsored anti-subversion rider which was anathema to the upper chamber.

Under House Rule X, clause 2, the Speaker appoints House conference managers. And by tradition, Senate managers are named by the Vice President or President pro tem of the Senate. However, the customary practice in both houses is for the chairman of the relevant committee to send to the desk a "little pink slip" bearing the names of his choices for the conference. The number of conferees is also determined by the committee chairman; this number, as we shall see, can be an important element in bargaining strategy.

Within the conference committee itself, an informal atmosphere prevails, encouraged by the fact that no minutes or formal records are kept of these sessions. "Participants,

2. Gilbert Y. Steiner, *The Congressional Conference Committee,* Illinois Studies in the Social Sciences, *32* (Urbana, University of Illinois Press, 1951). Steiner (pp. 7–13) outlines the mechanics of conferences in a thoroughgoing manner.

secure in the knowledge that there is no indisputable means of revealing their performance, may be more candid in expressing their true position and quicker to desert that which they are charged to uphold. They may threaten, cajole and bargain more directly than could be possible were a written record maintained."[3] In 1964 most of the senators and representatives interviewed appeared to enjoy the opportunity to practice the persuasive art in conference. "Here, the individual senator or congressman exercises maximum power," stated a senior member of the Senate committee. "Tremendous influence works here, and rank is of little importance compared to parliamentary skill and persuasive capacity."

Secrecy is an important shield for conferees against pressures from the outside. In the case of appropriations conferees, another shield protects the negotiators from pressure exerted by the President or party leaders. Because of the speed with which appropriations must be enacted at the end of a session, there is little opportunity for a party leader to establish strong lines of communication with an appropriations conferee.[4]

As Woodrow Wilson rather bitterly pointed out, conference reports are considered matters of high privilege in both House and Senate. In general, they are in order except (1) when the body is dividing or (2) when the *Journal* is being read. Partial reports may be accepted in both chambers. In such cases, approval is bestowed upon that portion of the report on which agreement has been reached in conference. Then the respective houses indicate whether they want their managers to insist further, whether they are willing to retreat, or whether they wish to propose another route to agreement.

3. Clapp, *The Congressman,* p. 284.
4. Huitt, "Congressional Organization and Operations," p. 436.

Floor discussion of the details of conference negotiations is rare, and the recommendations of the conference committee are usually accepted without fanfare. In the field of appropriations, the expertise of the conferees is respected; legislators outside the appropriations committees (or even those outside the relevant subcommittees) are unwilling to dispute the judgment of budgetary "experts." Furthermore, appropriations conference reports come up at the end of a session when government agencies badly need money and when congressmen are anxious to adjourn.

Budgetary politics can be traumatic. Consider this report of an appropriations conference, related by a staff member of the Senate Appropriations Committee:

> Let me tell you about the foreign aid conference. The chairman of the House group was Otto Passman . . . he fights aid strongly, and he's a real actor about it. In conference, he'll put on a big front . . . In his opening statement, he'll say that the House had extensive hearings, and that foreign aid appropriations are his *life* . . . Then he waves his hands and jumps up and down. The senators reply that a bicameral legislature must take into account the views of both houses. They'll try to calm Passman down. "Let's work out an acceptable bill," they'll say. Then they'll go to work to weaken Passman's position . . . they'll work on the principle of divide and conquer.

Not all appropriations conferences are this eventful, but they *are* all important. For they must end in agreement if federal bureaus are to receive money for governmental operations.

Like relations within each committee, the relations between the committees are characterized by lack of partisanship. A House staff member remarked that "the House and Senate groups stay together. Very seldom does partisanship break through." This impression was confirmed by a Senate subcommittee chairman who remarked that, although "you all negotiate," you "vote as a unit . . . not much partisanship is evident." As issues arise, each group retires to a back room and conducts a vote on whether to yield. After the vote, committee members are expected to maintain group loyalty.

An interesting question now arises: How can group unity best be maintained in conference? Clarence Cannon felt that a large group of conference representatives was more difficult to keep together than a small one. Therefore, he altered the tradition that required the House committee to be represented in conference by the entire subcommittee (six to nine members) handling a particular bill. Under Cannon's revised system, only five members would represent the House in conference (always including Cannon himself, just to ensure that nothing could go wrong).

A Republican member of the House committee voiced his admiration for the Cannon strategy: "I think that the number of House conferees should be limited to five. Five men are hard to divide and conquer. The senators can't chip off as many people as they used to." On the other side, a Senate staff member agreed, sadly, that the new House system was effective: "Hayden will usually take seven to nine members to conference, and the House has five members, to eliminate the divide and conquer strategy. You see—the more members there are, the rougher it is on the chairman." Conference committee behavior, including such elements as the "Cannon strategy," is extremely interesting. Yet political scientists have not done extensive work in this field. In 1951, however, a study *was* made of behavior in congressional conference committees (including appropriations conferences).

THE STEINER APPROACH

In *The Congressional Conference Committee,* Gilbert Y. Steiner sets out to accomplish a huge task. From an examination of the behavior of conference committees on agricultural, fiscal, security, welfare, appropriations, and labor legislation, Steiner attempts to answer the question: Which branch of the national legislature has been more effective in influencing the final form of legislation? For the purposes of this study, Steiner's analysis of appropriations conferences is most relevant.

Five appropriations meetings between the two committees are analyzed:

1. *Post Office and Treasury Department Appropriation of 1928.* In this case, Senator Bruce (an ardent wet) proposed an amendment increasing funds for prohibition enforcement from $13.5 million to $270.6 million. The Senate accepted the amendment, but the House was successful in deleting it in conference.

2. *First Deficiency Appropriation, 1929.* Another Senate attempt to increase prohibition enforcement funds was defeated by the House.

3. *Second Deficiency Appropriation, 1929.* The House emerged triumphant in a battle to block funds for the Nicaraguan Canal.

4. *Independent Offices Appropriation, 1933.* A Senate attempt to raise veterans' pensions above the amount requested by the President was defeated by the House. In this battle, the House conferees were aided by pressure exerted in their behalf by President Franklin D. Roosevelt.

5. *Urgent Deficiency Appropriation, 1943.* The House

committee had approved a resolution authorizing a sub-committee of the Appropriations Committee to examine allegations that certain federal employees had been, or were, members of subversive organizations. Because money was critically needed for government to function, the Senate conferees reluctantly acceded to House demands.

Steiner remarks that "it seems highly questionable that Senate bargaining power is necessarily any stronger or weaker in appropriation matters than in any other area. The ultimate question seems to be how determined the Senate is that there shall be legislation."[5] But in his conclusion Steiner is less cautious. Now he is ready to concede superior strength to the House appropriations conferees: "The fact that House influence was predominant in all cases of revenue and appropriations acts studied is possibly indicative of a determination to carry out the inference in the Constitution that the House should lead in making policy in this area."[6]

Actually, the observation of House "predominance" in these appropriations conferences stems largely from Steiner's selection of conferences. The Senate prohibition amendment, which was proposed in 1928, merely represented an attempt by a "wet" senator to embarrass the "drys" by forcing them to vote on an exorbitant sum for enforcement. Thus, the amendment was never expected to be retained in conference; House victory was assured. In the 1933 bill, House conferees were again successful—this time in limiting the amount to be appropriated for veterans' pensions. But in this case, the House was aided by the prestige and pressure which flowed from the White House. Finally, in 1943, the House won on the anti-subversion rider because the senators were unwilling

5. Steiner, p. 72.
6. Ibid., p. 172.

to provoke an argument which would delay the appropriation of desperately needed agency funds.

Thus, it would seem that Steiner's results do not justify an assertion of House predominance in appropriations conferences. For, in his examples, special circumstances assured House victories. (A recent study by Fenno, covering thirty-six bureaus for the period 1947–62, shows the Senate winning more frequently than the House. This should caution us against accepting a statement about House predominance.)

Not only does Steiner's study concern itself with too few appropriations conferences, it also fails to distinguish adequately between them. Conferences are really confrontations between pairs of House and Senate *subcommittees* considering a piece of legislation—and the relationships between various sets of subcommittees differ widely from each other. Some subcommittee sets (like Defense) are well-known for the cordiality prevailing between Senate and House groups, while others (like Legislative Appropriations) have often been the focal points for severe conflict. In certain cases, this relationship turns on the question of personalities. For example, the close relationship between Senator Saltonstall and Representative Mahon helps to make Military Construction conferences friendly. On the other hand, the personal bitterness between Senator Russell and Representative Whitten has disrupted Agriculture Appropriations conferences in the past. Reported one senator: "We all stood behind Russell in his personal argument with Jamie Whitten in Agriculture; they stood behind Whitten. Both sides were absolutely unbending."

Although it is true that the Senate subcommittees frequently increase House allotments, this relationship "varies with the agency, the issue area, and the particular item."[7]

7. Wildavsky, *The Politics of the Budgetary Process,* p. 52.

For Representative Walt Horan, as we have seen, forestry had become a "religion"; the congressman saw himself as the protector of the Forestry Service. A Senate staff assistant remembers a case in which a Senate Appropriations subcommittee *reduced* the amount appropriated by the House:

> I remember the 1958 conference on the State Department appropriations bill. The Republican director of the USIA, [Arthur] Larson, had gone to Hawaii for a Lincoln Day celebration. He made a highly political speech, in which he said that, from 1932 to 1952, our government was in the grip of an alien philosophy. The Democrats, of course, resented this. He'd requested $140 million and the House cut him to $113 million . . . Then Senator Fulbright operated on Larson, and he came out with $85 million for his agency.

In a study of appropriations conferences in depth, one would have to account for the differences between agencies in terms of the degree of success achieved. It is not enough to say that the Senate subcommittees are more generous than are their counterparts in the House. Rather, we must ask: Why does a *particular program* fare better in one house than in the other? For example, Wildavsky shows that the Senate is usually more generous than the House in natural resource matters because the interests desiring increased appropriations in this area are better represented in the Senate. The fact that the Reclamation Bureau works in seventeen western states means that it has a much greater voice in the Senate than in the House, where a smaller percentage of representatives are directly affected.

A study of comparative strength of the two houses in appropriations conferences should examine each pair of subcommittees separately. Because the pattern varies so widely from one subcommittee set to another, it is practically impossible to speak of House or Senate "predominance" in all appropriations matters. Rather, a study must examine comparative strength in, let's say, Defense Appropriations conferences or Foreign Operations conferences. First, it is useful to determine whether the final dollar amount agreed upon is closer to the House or Senate figure. But an evaluation of "comparative strength" must go beyond a mere examination of money figures. The results of bargaining over *wording* must also be considered in order to determine who has "won" a conference battle. This could be done by a perusal of conference reports together with a reading of relevant portions of the *Congressional Record,* which might show why each house insisted on its own particular wording. Such a reading might also tell us how intensely a particular chamber felt about an amendment, and how great a "commitment" had been made by the conferees. This study will not attempt such a close analysis of comparative House–Senate strength in conferences (which might easily fill a volume by itself), but will consider some of the *strategies* used by the participants to gain their preferred ends.

COMMON AND DIVERGENT INTERESTS

The conference relations between the appropriations committees of the House and Senate are often characterized by tension and bitterness. But this does not necessarily mean that we are dealing with a pure conflict situation, in which one committee's gain is the other's loss. For there may be common interests which unite the two committees and which increase the tendency for each to seek compromise with the other. As one Senate committee member remarked, "Conference is a procedure of compromise, and like in any compromise, there is give and take. Compromise is the method of getting legislation and it is difficult for new members to get used to this." On the House side, a member spoke of a specific case which showed that—no matter how tenaciously positions are held—bargaining is possible: "In conference we've had a fight on the welfare for the District of Columbia. There is a question on aid to children of unemployed parents. Senator Bob Byrd is opposed; the House is in favor. Although Byrd is very adamant, *you do bargain.*"

Appropriations conferences are, indeed, bargaining situations. One committee's gain is not simply the other's loss; there are common interests as well as opposing ones between the two bodies. In *The Strategy of Conflict*, Thomas C. Schelling describes situations in which conflict is mixed with mutual dependence:

> These are the "games" in which, though the element of conflict provides the dramatic interest, mutual dependence is part of the logical structure and demands some kind of collaboration or mutual accommodation—tacit, if not explicit—even if only in the avoidance of mutual disaster.[8]

What in the appropriations process makes agreement between the two bodies necessary, makes "mutual dependence" part of the "logical structure" of the game?

A senior member of the Senate committee provides the answer: "You iron things out . . . each side realizes that you have to concede something. There is the knowledge that there ultimately has to be a bill." But why is stalemate distasteful to the appropriating legislators? Do the senators and congressmen have something to lose if an appropriations bill is stalled in conference? A few of the results of such a deadlock might indeed seem upsetting to a member of Congress: When an appropriations deadlock occurs, as it did in 1962,

8. Thomas C. Schelling, *The Strategy of Conflict* (New York, Oxford University Press, Galaxy Books, 1963), p. 83.

the appropriations committees lose prestige both in Congress and in the country at large. For men who take a great deal of pride in their budgetary work and who value their reputations as "responsible" legislators, it is disquieting indeed to become the target of such widespread public and journalistic disapproval as was heaped upon them in 1962. It is also embarrassing to the appropriations committee leaders to have party chiefs like Senator Mansfield and Representative Albert intervene (as they did in 1962) in order to break up a budgetary log-jam. Appropriations leaders, after all, like to feel that they can "run their own show."

For members of a majority party trying to enact its own Administration's program, an appropriations rift can be especially disturbing. One Democrat on the House committee remarked: "Cannon favored a resolution blasting the Senate, but Sidney Yates [Congressman from Illinois] and I objected to the resolution. The situation . . . was not good for the Democratic party."

A final reason why "there has to be a bill" might be that appropriations committee members in both houses do not wish to see government defense, foreign aid, and education programs starved for funds. As prime actors in the political arena, appropriations legislators know that they are playing a crucial part in the formulation of public policy. They do not want to be responsible for the collapse of government.

For all these reasons—pride in Congress and in the appropriations process, party loyalty (in the case of the party supporting the Administration), and an unwillingness to carry on total war against government operations—members of the House and Senate Appropriations Committees have a certain common interest in reaching an agreement in conference committee. Now we must see how this is done. "Conference is a matter of horse-trading," says one senior senator, and a House committee member adds: "In conference you try to outwait and out-talk each other." What kinds of strategies are used by each side to gain its ends in "horse trading" with the other?

CONFERENCE STRATEGIES: THE "COMMITMENT"

Schelling outlines several strategies that serve useful purposes in contests involving participants who have certain shared (as well as opposing) interests. A few of his "strategies" proved to be particularly applicable to appropriations conferences of recent years. The theories Schelling presents helped to bring a measure of analytical coherence to the wide variety of strategies described both in the literature and in interview sessions, and also suggested new relations which were the subjects of further questions to congressmen.

One interesting element of conference strategy is suggested by Schelling in the following passage:

> The well-known principle that one should pick good negotiators to represent him and then give them complete flexibility and authority—a principle commonly voiced by negotiators themselves—is by no means as self-evident as its proponents suggest; the power of a negotiator often rests on a manifest inability to make concessions and to meet demands.[9]

In this case, one side may increase its bargaining power by *depriving* itself of the power to act. A conference team might take an adamant position, thus giving notice that it will not back down. "We *can't* back down; we've committed ourselves." Thus, the conferees from the other house are forced to give in if government activity is to continue.

In past Congresses, conference teams have sought "instruc-

9. Ibid., p. 19.

tions" from their own house which would bind the negotiators to a specific stand. In 1933, the Senate attempted to resist White House pressure on the Independent Offices bill by declaring that the conferees were "instructed" to stand by certain amendments. And in the middle of the furious controversy surrounding the Urgent Deficiency Appropriations of 1943, Senator McKellar sought "guidance" from the upper house in the form of a vote. The Senate responded by giving its conferees a 69–0 mandate to hold firm at the Senate position.[10] By committing themselves to a position and by showing that "even if we did surrender, our house wouldn't accept the bill," a group of conferees can gain a powerful bargaining advantage.

Often, the Senate or House will include in a bill items to which the body is *not* committed. Sacrificing these, the negotiators will attempt to stand fast by all "commitments." This seems fair—"we surrender on some points and hold on others." Actually, of course, many of the "expendable" items were included merely for bargaining purposes. A high-ranking House member noted that "the Senate will up measures and then expect that they will be taken out in conference." On the other side, House subcommittees make cuts which they know will be restored when the conferees meet. In bargaining, each side starts from a more extreme position than it can realistically expect to hold. (The 1962 Senate claim to the right to initiate appropriations is an example of such a position; the solons could not, given the crowded nature of their schedules, initiate appropriations. Nevertheless, they used this "demand" for bargaining purposes.)

As Schelling points out, "a potent means of commitment, and sometimes the only means, is the pledge of one's reputation. If national representatives can arrange to be charged

10. Steiner, pp. 67, 69.

with appeasement for every small concession, they place concession visibly beyond their own reach."[11] Both houses of Congress are proud groups, and they often view a conference battle as a test of power and prestige between the two bodies. In 1929, a House member described a conference victory in glowing terms: "The House has just won a notable victory for the cause of good government . . . This body always has been and is now the conservative, sane legislative body that protects the Treasury of the United States and is at the call of the cause of good government at any time."[12]

On the Senate side, the honor of the legislative body is also held sacred. Consider Senator Green's speech on the subject of the Deficiency Appropriations conference in 1943:

> I think the Senate of the United States will have fallen quite low if it abandons a matter of principle . . . merely because a group of conferees refuses to take a question back to the House. In other words, if the small number represented by the conferees . . . is to be unreasonable and is to refuse to take the matter back to the House when it has been voted by the Senate three times, it seems to me we shall be groveling at the feet of the House of Representatives.[13]

When a group of conferees has become "committed" to a position, and when that group is backed up by an angry parent body unwilling to concede a matter of principle, the conferees have a definite bargaining advantage.

An extreme tactic is the threat of "mutual destruction."[14] In 1943, for example, the House threatened to bury the entire Deficiency Appropriations bill unless the Senate would

11. Schelling, p. 29.
12. Steiner, p. 64.
13. Ibid., p. 71.
14. Schelling, p. 23.

agree to its "anti-subversive" amendment. The representatives' threatened sabotage of the conference, which would mean the defeat of both houses' versions of the bill and the denial of funds to federal agencies, proved to be a valuable bargaining tool; the senators finally acceded to House demands.

One qualification must be made in listing this destructive strategy as a useful one in appropriations conferences: The matter involved must be of such importance that one house can convince the other that surrender on this point would be more painful for the threatening committee than would a breakdown in the appropriations process, with the consequent public scorn and party leaders' interference. To be *effective*, a threat must be *credible*.

According to Schelling, a tradition of successful bargaining in the past is helpful in facilitating the resolution of conflict in the present. Here is one way in which a history of past negotiations is useful:

> Bargaining can only occur when at least one party takes initiative in proposing a bargain. A deterrent to initiative is the information it yields, or may seem to yield, about one's eagerness. But if each has visible reason to expect the other to meet him halfway, because of a history of successful bargaining, that very history provides protection against the inference of overeagerness.[15]

As in international relations, a history of close communication and successful bargaining between two appropriations subcommittees helps to make agreement easier in the future and minimizes the chances for disturbances in the process. In this case, neither side need feel overly cautious about initiating suggestions for agreement. There is a reasonable

15. Ibid., p. 46.

expectation that the other side will meet the initiating side "halfway."

Some subcommittees enjoy such a long history of coopera- tion and negotiation that their meetings become quite in- formal. One senator remarked that "George Mahon and I do most of our conference business over golf at Burning Tree —even though he's a good golfer and I'm not. The other day, George told me—informally—'take that goddamn lan- guage out of the bill; it's too abrasive.' He got the word 'abra- sive' from Bobby Kennedy."

As a tradition of negotiations in the past facilitates bar- gaining in the present, so the prospect of future meetings adds a new dimension to the conference situation. Schelling points out that the prospect of future negotiations can make con- cession more difficult, as each side strives to maintain an image of "firmness" which will continue into the future. Actually, the 1964 interviews showed the expectation of future appropriations conferences making accommodation *easier*. Concessions can be made in one year with the under- standing that the other house will repay the favor in the next session. A congressman's description of conference behavior illustrates this point:

> You will recall the situation with respect to the two
> ——— [installations] . . . For the past three years they
> have been knocked out of the House bill on a point of
> order and then, in the Senate, Senator ——— has gotten
> the one in his state back in the bill. Then it goes to
> conference. This year the House conferees said they
> would not go along with that provision; the Senate
> conferees said they had to go along . . . The Senator
> concerned was engaged in a primary the day after the
> conference was supposed to break up, and it was argued
> he should be protected. We went along but with the

solemn pledge of every House conferee speaking directly to all Senate conferees: "This is the last year for this item and we want you to know it." . . . It will never be approved again and they know it.[16]

Like a *history* of negotiations, the prospect of *future* negotiations can aid conferees in reaching an agreement in the present. Irrevocable conflict this year may be staved off by promises made for the future.

"Natural Meeting Point"

Having isolated a number of strategies which might be used by participants in appropriations conferences, we must now ask what determines the point at which agreement is finally made. Schelling suggests that conflicts are "solved" when the two contesting parties coordinate their expectations concerning an optimal final outcome.[17] Most situations present a natural "clue" or "meeting point" which offers itself as a key to agreement. Among all the available options, some particular one usually seems to be the focal point for co-ordinated choice. Schelling applies this theory to tacit bargaining situations and says that there is "abundant evidence" that such "natural meeting points" also influence behavior in explicit bargaining situations.

Appropriations conferences normally involve bargaining between teams advocating two different sums of money.

In bargains that involve numerical magnitudes . . . there seems to be a strong magnetism in mathematical simplicity. A trivial illustration is the tendency for the outcomes to be expressed in "round numbers" . . . The frequency with which final agreement is precipitated by an offer to "split the difference" illustrates the same

16. Clapp, p. 286.
17. Schelling, pp. 53 ff.

point, and the difference that is split is by no means always trivial.[18]

Many of the legislators interviewed mentioned "splitting the difference" as a common method of resolving conference disputes; one senator explained that this was a time-saving device for his committee.

"Splitting it down the middle" can be done by agreeing on a figure halfway between the Senate- and House-proposed amounts. But the even split can be achieved in another way: "In Independent Offices, Al Thomas is a great negotiator. He says—'split, split, split: House yields here, Senate yields there' . . . Goes really fast. You have to say 'Stop it, Al.'" The late Representative Albert Thomas, who was Chairman of the Independent Offices subcommittee of the House Appropriations Committee until his death in 1966, might have appeared to do the splitting in a fair way: one item for the House, one for the Senate. But when the splitting was over, the senators were sometimes unpleasantly surprised to find that their group had conceded on large items while the House had surrendered on small ones.

Adding a Twist to Schelling's Theory

When relations between subcommittees are amicable, then Schelling's "split the difference" formula appears to be a useful one. But, as one senior senator remarked, "it all depends on the mood of the conference itself." If the prestige of the two houses is at stake, it is possible that each side will seek to reach agreement at a place slightly on its own side of the "middle" point. Here is one congressmen's tale of this kind of conference activity:

Last year there was a difference of about $400 million between the House and Senate versions of the foreign

18. Ibid., p. 67.

aid appropriation. The chairman of the House delegation in the conference took a very firm position that we had to end up with slightly less than 50 per cent of the difference as a matter of prestige. It was the day we were to adjourn. We were in conference until about 10:30 P.M., and the Senate wouldn't give in. I think the difference between conferees was only five or ten million dollars. The Senate was fighting for its prestige, and our chairman for his. At 10:30 he started to close his book and got up saying he would get instructions from the House. All the rest of our conferees did the same. That prospect was too much for the Senators. They capitulated.[19]

Thus, the House was able to force an agreement on *its* side of the "self-evident meeting place" by threatening to use a strategy of "commitment"—by threatening to throw the weight of the House against foreign aid and thus to tie the hands of the conferees.

Schelling's model is a useful tool in pointing out strategies used by contestants in appropriations conferences. In certain cases, the theories set forth in *The Strategy of Conflict* may be slightly modified to fit the budgetary process. For example, Schelling sees the prospect of continuing negotiations primarily as a hardening force on the negotiators; each side will wish to maintain an image of unbending strength. However, as we have seen, the promise of further negotiations may also aid agreement in conferences by providing an opportunity for future repayment of present concessions.

Further, Schelling's notion that contestants will strive to reach agreement at a self-evident meeting place may be adapted to reflect differing circumstances. If the subcommittees are on friendly terms, then they might well meet at

19. Clapp, p. 281.

the halfway point. But if relations between the two are bitter
—or if the matter has become a test of prestige between the
chambers—then each committee may strive to secure a final
agreement on its own side of the self-evident meeting place.

As we have seen in Chapter 2, congressional budgetary decisions are made in an incremental manner, dealing with one
small part of the budget at a time. Moreover, the decisions
are not all made in one central body. Rather, decision-
making is carried on simultaneously in various centers within
Congress: some decisions are made in the House, some in
the Senate, some in authorizing committees and others in
appropriations committees. No comprehensive plan directs
congressional work on the budget; there is an endless sequence of experimental policy moves. Starting from the
status quo as a base, budgetary decision-makers in Congress
change policy gradually as new experience throws new light
on what is desirable and what is politically possible.

But what functions does the conference committee serve
in budgetary decision-making? How does the resolution of
House–Senate differences help legislators to understand the
budget and to bring influence to bear on it? Finally, what is
the effect of such conference resolution on the formulation
of public policy?

First of all, it appears that the conference is an important
step in the incremental consideration of the budget. As we
have seen, it would be impossible for legislators to consider
the budget as a whole—studying all alternatives and their
possible consequences for public policy. The problems of
calculation would be so vast that one would not know where
to begin. But the conference limits the range of calculation

by focusing the legislators' attention on the *differences* between Senate and House bills.

In this way, the senators and representatives can concentrate their attention on manageable sections of the budget. Furthermore, these sections represent important, politically sensitive portions of the budget. They are largely made up of funds which have been granted by the Senate committee to appealing agencies whose requests had been slashed by the House. It would be of less value to the legislators to study appropriations about which both houses are in agreement; conferences limit the focus of attention to those appropriations that are the subjects of dispute.

Conferences serve still another purpose in budgetary decision-making, that of *coordinating* decisions made at separate power centers—the Senate and House Appropriations Committees. Lindblom discusses various types of coordination. The one most useful for this study is "partisan mutual adjustment," wherein "adjustments to each other are made by decision-makers who . . . differ in the values they think important."[20] The Senate and House Appropriations Committees certainly hold some differing values, but the two groups must make adjustments to each other. For if they do not reach agreement, the appropriations process comes to a halt.

Considering Lindblom's categories of adjustment patterns, it does not seem that the committees coordinate decisions in an "atomistic" manner (in which each group simply ignores the repercussions of its decisions on other groups). Nor is the pattern "deferential"; although the Senate committee allows its House counterpart to initiate spending bills, it

20. Charles E. Lindblom, "Decision-Making in Taxation and Expenditures," in *Public Finances: Needs, Sources and Utilization,* A Conference of the Universities–National Bureau Committee For Economic Research (Princeton, Princeton University Press, 1961), p. 313.

does not defer to House judgment in conference. Rather, the coordination achieved by appropriations conferences appears to be closer to what Lindblom calls *strategic* partisan mutual adjustment. "In this method, decision-makers manipulate each other in a variety of ways. They may do so by partisan discussion . . . by exchange of effective threats and promises."[21] The appropriations committees of the upper and lower houses certainly engage in partisan discussion, as they argue en route to their final place of accommodation. They also exchange threats (of mutual destruction) and promises (of concession at a future meeting).

This model suggests a function for appropriations conferences in budgetary decision-making: Conferences coordinate separate decision-making centers by providing an arena for bargaining between two opposing decision-making groups. Partisan mutual adjustment achieves coordination without relying on a single unit which must consider the budget as a whole.

Lindblom outlines the ways in which such coordination achieves desirable results. First of all, partisan mutual adjustment is a process through which values important to a particular group can influence policy-making. (For example, agencies can make their views felt in conference by briefing the Senate conferees on their requests and by applying pressure on the senators.) Furthermore, such adjustment often achieves a satisfactory weighting of conflicting values and competing claims. However, this is true only if we accept the notion that a "satisfactory" weighting gives an advantage to programs with political appeal. As one House staff member remarked: "The appeal of a program is all-important. The National Institutes of Health is very appealing to people, in that they hope they can find answers to medical

21. Ibid., p. 315.

problems. Everybody around here has a relative who has cancer or heart trouble." But some governmental units like the United States Information Agency have had extremely difficult sledding in the appropriations process because they have not been able to gain support from groups in society to the same degree that N.I.H. has. Lindblom's analysis does not show how such programs as foreign aid and USIA can secure a generous share of the budgetary pie if they do not have strong group support. And such agencies cannot be passed over easily, for they are important instruments of modern foreign policy.

Partisan mutual adjustment helps record the demands of various interest groups by allowing them to register their preferences in the bargaining situation. The House committee may be seen as representing those segments of the American public who would like to cut government spending, while the Senate stands as the negotiator for federal agencies and for the people who benefit from their services. Those programs which have the widest appeal will probably be successful, and those interests which are held most intensely will find a hearing in conference. As Lindblom says, "A supporting hypothesis is that policy will respond relatively more to widely shared and/or intensely held values than to less widely shared and/or less intensely held values and that, consequently, values will in effect often be weighted in a satisfactory way."[22]

It is, however, possible that those programs with the widest and most intense constituency backing are not those which are most beneficial to the nation as a whole. But this is terribly difficult to prove; we are led to normative notions of what makes good public policy. In the Lindblom scheme groups *do* feel represented. However, there may be programs

22. Ibid., p. 317.

which are beneficial but which do not attract group support. In 1964, for example, Congress refused to print additional copies of the Surgeon General's report on smoking—because a strong interest group, the tobacco farmers, opposed it. Perhaps we could modify Lindblom's theory to say that good public policy would emerge from partisan mutual adjustment only if groups and individuals had access to all the information bearing on a subject. But how could we be sure that those who had the information would then choose the "right" policies? We are again doomed to frustration; it is difficult to deal with this point scientifically.

Lindblom's analysis is useful in two ways. First, it helps us to identify the appropriations conference as the place in which incremental budgetary decisions undertaken in two diverse power centers are coordinated. We can see the conference as the place of bargaining between the House committee, representing the interests of thrift and economy in society, and the Senate committee, representing the various government agencies and their constituents. Out of this confrontation and compromise comes a public policy which must take into account both the interests of the economizers and the interests of those who manage and benefit from government programs.

Secondly, the Lindblom analysis alerts us to a possible danger in the creation of a Joint Budgetary Committee. For in maintaining diverse power centers, the appropriations process provides various interested groups with access to the budgetary system. Both economic conservatives and supporters of welfare programs are able to make their influence felt on policy. If a Joint Appropriations Committee attempted to formulate a coherent budget without allowing this conflict and play of interests to take place, an appropriations measure might emerge which did not take into account the political preferences of society. The economizers would not feel as comfortable without a strong House committee to defend their views, and the agencies would, no doubt, be unhappy to find that their court of appeals was gone.

But why does conflict arise between the two committees? And what are the results of such battles? Chapter 5 will take up these two problems: the causes and consequences of appropriations wars.

5

THE CAUSES AND CONSEQUENCES

OF CONFLICT

The Congressional banana war between the House
and Senate Appropriations Committees continued
this week . . . Since April, Mr. Cannon has kept the
door to the Treasury locked for all governmental
agencies. Two weeks after the 1963 fiscal year began,
not a dime has been appropriated for any of them.
> Tom Wicker, "House vs. Senate"
> in The New York Times, *July 15,*
> *1962.*

The clash of doctrines is not a disaster, it is an
opportunity.
> *Alfred North Whitehead,* Science
> and the Modern World.[1]

THE CAUSES OF CONFLICT: UPPER HOUSE VS. LOWER HOUSE

Earl Latham has remarked that "even within the structure
of official agencies in one branch of the federal government
competition of group interests takes place. Mention has
been made of the consciousness of a separate group interest
as between the two houses of Congress."[2] The House and

1. Quoted in Lewis A. Coser, *The Functions of Social Conflict* (New
York, Free Press of Glencoe, 1956), p. 9.
2. Earl Latham, *The Group Basis of Politics* (Ithaca, Cornell University Press, 1952), pp. 45–46.

Senate do indeed maintain proudly separate group identities, and they struggle for independent group interests.

One clear source of the 1962 split was a struggle for power and prestige between the Senate and House. The *New York Times* declared that "the shooting all started because Mr. Cannon and his numerous adherents in the House of Representatives decided that the Senate does not treat their chamber with sufficient respect."[3] House members, annoyed at the publicity and attention lavished on their brethren in the upper house, tend to view the right to initiate appropriations (and the right to exercise the dominant power in the appropriations process) as a sacred preserve of the House of Representatives. In this field, at least, representatives can be the leaders. One member of the House committee remarked: "The houses are very jealous of prerogatives. The House is strong on the idea of its rights to appropriate. A tradition has grown up, and it is extremely jealously guarded. We all fight off any kind of encroachment." As might have been predicted, the House was accorded harsher treatment at the hands of a senior member of the Senate committee: "The House recognizes its inferior status everywhere except for this. The places of meeting did not constitute a real dispute. They were drummed up."

Since the late 1950s, the study of conflict has received the attention of a growing number of social scientists. In *The Functions of Social Conflict* Lewis A. Coser distills from the theories of Georg Simmel a series of basic propositions about conflict. One states that:

> Before a social conflict between negatively and positively privileged groups can take place, before hostile attitudes are turned into social action, the negatively privileged group must first develop the awareness that it is, indeed,

3. *New York Times,* July 15, 1962.

negatively privileged. It must come to believe that it is being denied rights to which it is entitled.[4]

Although it has often been observed that the Senate has gained power at the expense of the House, this fact alone would not automatically lead to a clash between the houses. For it would first be necessary for the House to realize that it is negatively privileged. The words of one congressman are instructive on this point:

> There is no comparison in the way House and Senate members get inflated. Part of the explanation is the attention the Senate gets in the press; part of it is the huge buildup in staff they have, and the fact they are elected for six-year terms. The House member doesn't delude himself that the world is watching his every move. Every senator seems to feel his great sovereignty.[5]

Many of my (and of Charles Clapp's) House interviewees referred to the greater degree of power, prestige, and publicity which they felt was bestowed upon the upper house. This would suggest that the "negatively-privileged" group is indeed aware that it is negatively privileged. On Coser's terms, conflict may result from such perception.

Discussing "hostility and tensions in conflict relationships," Coser makes an interesting distinction:

> Conflicts which arise from frustration of specific demands within the relationship and from estimates of gains of the participants, and which are directed at the presumed frustrating object, can be called *realistic conflicts,* insofar as they are means toward a specific result. *Non-realistic conflicts,* on the other hand, although still

4. Coser, p. 37.
5. Clapp, *The Congressman,* p. 40.

involving interactions between two or more persons, are not occasioned by the rival ends of the antagonists, but by the need for tension release of at least one of them.[6]

In analyzing the 1962 clash between committees, many observers were amazed that the chairmanship of a conference committee or the place of a meeting could make up the core issue of a battle which split apart two powerful legislative units. One explanation might be that the House committee really did not consider the walk to the Senate side of the Capitol a major issue. Rather, the 1962 outburst was a method of releasing tension and resentment against the senators—a resentment which had been building up through the years.

A closely related explanation is that the House committee was pugnacious because it wanted to assert its own independence and the independence of its parent body against the claims of the upper house.[7] In order to explain the 1962 conflict, one does not have to prove that the issue of the meeting place was in itself an important one. Rather, this issue symbolized for House members the unfair domination exercised by senators in relations between the houses and also symbolized the prestige enjoyed by the upper house. In the continuing struggle for status and power between the two houses of Congress lies one important root of appropriations conflict.

It is now necessary to examine the appropriations committees themselves in order to discover additional sources of

6. Coser, p. 49.

7. Karl Deutsch has written: "Men may decide to fight about an issue not on its merits but because of its function as a symbol of their own integrity. In such cases they may feel that a showdown is impending on the question of their independence." "Mass Communications and the Loss of Freedom in National Decision-Making; A Possible Research Approach," *Journal of Conflict Resolution, 1* (June 1957), 200.

conflict. The committees' interdependence—the fact that agreement is needed between the two bodies before appropriations can be made—makes their relationship particularly sensitive.

GROUP IDEOLOGY AND SOCIALIZATION

How does group membership influence an individual's perception of the world around him?

> It appears . . . that the group experiences and affiliations of an individual are the primary, though not the exclusive, means by which the individual knows, interprets and reacts to the society in which he exists. Their significance here is that they produce in their participants certain uniformities of behavior and attitude that must be achieved by the individual if he is to be a completely accepted member of the group. The process by which the individual readies these uniformities is essentially what is meant by the term socialization. These uniformities, moreover, cover, and in a sense regulate, the whole range of man's attitudes towards groups of which he is not a member.[8]

Organizations, for the purpose of simplification, project for their members a view of the world which is filled with stereotypes: "good guys" and "bad guys." Conflicts between organizations do not involve a struggle over "brute facts," but derive rather from the element of "perceived hostility." That is, one group will oppose another if the shared "image" of the first group shows the second as the perpetrator of improper acts. The facts themselves are not as important as the groups' *perception* of them.

8. David B. Truman, *The Governmental Process* (New York, Alfred A. Knopf, 1955), p. 21.

In the light of this theory, it is possible to locate another source of conflict in the appropriations process. For the "images" of the House and Senate Appropriations Committees, the shared ideologies of each committee, are in conflict with each other. In July 1962, each appropriations committee adopted a resolution which pointed up its own particular view of the world. On July 6 the Senate committee declared that the federal government should not be "endangered" by "unreasonable demands for the surrender of the Senate to the will of the other body." Clearly, the Senate committee felt that it was the protector of stable government against the irresponsible attacks of the House committee. The representatives replied on July 9 that "in the past 10 years the Senate conferees have been able to retain $22 billion out of the $32 billion in increases which the Senate added to House appropriations—a two-to-one ratio in favor of the body consistently advocating larger appropriations, increased spending and corresponding deficits."[9]

Seen through the eyes of a socialized House committee member, the Senate committee's advocacy of higher appropriations appears as irresponsible spending. On the other hand, a Senate committee member sees the House committee's cuts as electioneering devices, the exhibiting of false economy. ("We should just accept their cuts—boy, would they be panicked then!" remarked a Senate staff member.) The "objective" situation might not bear out the validity of either ideology but—as Boulding notes—"it is not the 'objective' situation which matters, but the subjective images of the participants."[10]

The socialization processes in each body, aided by systems

9. *Congressional Quarterly Weekly Report,* July 20, 1962, pp. 1226, 1238.

10. Kenneth E. Boulding, "Organization and Conflict," *Journal of Conflict Resolution, 1* (June 1957), 131.

of rewards and punishments, encourage committee members to think of their opposite numbers as somewhat tainted with irresponsibility. Much in the committee ideologies may be exaggerated, but certain elements are rooted in fact. The Senate Appropriations Committee does, in most cases, recommend higher amounts than does its House counterpart. And, because the committees' conflict is partially rooted in this divergence in behavior, it is relevant to ask the question: Why has the Senate committee been, through the years, more generous in appropriations than the House?

FACTORS FAVORING SENATE GENEROSITY

Constituency

"Well, it's all a difference in constituencies. Keating has to represent the whole state and Rooney only a small New York district." This was the explanation offered by a Senate staff member for the differences in appropriations behavior of the Senate and the House. Basically, the point is this: A House member, who represents only a segment of a state's population, can look out for his own constituents' needs and do the bidding of the small number of interests in his own territory. For all other groups, he need show no mercy. The senator, on the other hand, represents an entire state; he must serve as caretaker of the interests of a wider variety of groups. Representative Rooney of Brooklyn could easily work against appropriations for upstate New York interests. But Senator Keating's constituency included all of New York state. The senators, who must look out for a larger number of interests, will tend to advocate increased appropriations in many areas. Such behavior explains in part why the Senate's final appropriations figures are higher than those of the House.

86

Committee Structure

Another reason for the Senate's comparative generosity becomes apparent when the structure of the Senate committee is examined. The Chairman of the Agriculture Appropriations subcommittee is Spessard Holland, the third ranking Democrat on the Senate Agriculture and Forestry Committee. Richard Russell, Chairman of the Armed Services Committee, serves also as Chairman of the Defense Appropriations subcommittee; Carl Hayden sits on the Interior Committee and heads the Interior subcommittee on Appropriations. The list goes on. Senator Lister Hill, Chairman of the Committee on Labor and Public Welfare, is Chairman also of the Labor-Health, Education and Welfare Appropriations subcommittee. And A. Willis Robertson, who heads the Senate's Banking and Currency Committee, serves as Chairman of the Treasury Appropriations subcommittee.

The pattern is clear. Senate chairmen and members of appropriations subcommittees often serve concurrently as chairmen or high-ranking members of closely related substantive committees. Mr. Russell is chairman of the committee that authorizes Defense Department funds; he then chairs the group which decides how much of that amount to appropriate. Naturally, a man will rarely turn against the figures which his own committee has approved. (In the House, an Appropriations Committee member has no other committees. Therefore, there is no interlocking directorate —the man who appropriates cannot be the one who has authorized. As a result, slashes will be made more freely.)

The close relationship which exists between Senate authorizing and appropriating committees is strengthened by invitations offered to senatorial experts in various fields to sit as ex officio members of appropriations subcommittees. Allen J. Ellender, Chairman of the Agriculture Committee, is a member ex officio of the Agriculture subcommittee, while J. William Fulbright, Chairman of the Foreign Relations Committee, serves as an ex officio member of the State Department subcommittee when diplomatic and consular items are discussed. And Alan Bible, Chairman of the District of Columbia Committee, is invited to join the deliberations of the D.C. Appropriations subcommittee. Polsby remarks that "in the House money bills are seen primarily in the context of assaults on the Treasury; in the Senate they are seen as financial extensions of programs, as expressions of legitimate social and political demands."[11] The practice of inviting members of relevant authorizing committees to serve ex officio on appropriations subcommittees can help to form this Senate view, for the invited experts are able to explain how a particular expenditure fits into a broader program. Thus informed, the Senate subcommittee members may be less likely to make wholesale cuts than will their counterparts in the House, who do not have similar ties with the authorizing committees of their own body.

Sequence and Procedure

"It's a matter of calendar. We get the bills after the House gets them." Thus a conservative Senate committee member tries to explain why his group is more generous in appropriations than is the House committee. "The Senate should start initiating—the House might increase funds then," remarks a Senate staff aide. "The House cuts too deeply and the Senate corrects," adds a senior member of the Senate committee.

Interviews lead to the conclusion that senators really expect the House members to act first and to cut deeply. The senators, as we have seen, have no real desire to initiate ap-

11. Polsby, *Congress and the Presidency*, p. 96.

propriations. They merely react to House cuts. On the other side, the representatives realize that many of their cuts will be restored by the Senate. Therefore, the following of traditional sequence and traditional behavior by the participants tends to continue the established pattern of "Senate high and House low."

Because the Senate committee holds open hearings, Administration officials and lobbyists can exert more public pressure on the Senate group than they can on the House, which keeps most of its hearings closed to the public. A House committee member remarked that "if open, your committee is exposed to pressures. All kinds of pressures can develop on you." Perhaps the public pressure and high degree of publicity make it harder for senators to refuse the appropriations demands of interested groups.

Subcommittee Assignment

A final reason for Senate generosity is suggested by Robert A. Wallace.[12] In the House, majority members are appointed to subcommittees by the chairman; minority members are "nominated" by their ranking member and "confirmed" by the chairman. In the Senate, each member makes his own choice—subject to seniority. Thus, House subcommittee members are less likely to have a direct interest in the items considered. On a rivers and harbors bill where the Senate group was "stacked" with members personally interested in projects, but the House group was not, the Senate raised the House grant by 35 per cent. On an Interior appropriation under the same conditions the Senate increased the House figure by 15 per cent. But where *both* subcommittees

12. Robert A. Wallace, "Congressional Control of Federal Spending," *Midwest Journal of Political Science, 3* (May 1959), pp. 151–67.

were stacked in favor of agriculture appropriations, the Senate increase was less than one per cent.[13]

These, then, are some causes of conflict in the appropriations process: a power struggle between the two houses of Congress; patterns of socialization in each committee which lead to group ideologies hostile to the opposite committee; differences in constituency, committee structure, procedure, and method of subcommittee assignment.

What are the consequences of conflict? Mr. Wicker saw the appropriations conflict as a damaging experience for the executive branch. But must we not also consider Whitehead's assertion that the clash of doctrines can be an opportunity? Might some public good come from conflict in the appropriations process?

DISRUPTIVE CONSEQUENCES

On June 16, 1962, Secret Service Chief James J. Rowley sent a memorandum to some 700 Secret Service personnel asking them "to volunteer without any pay starting June 17." He wrote: "While I am not able to guarantee that you will be reimbursed for this voluntary service, I am confident that the appropriate authorities will see to it that you are paid in full for your service."[14] (It is illegal for a federal employee to work without pay unless he has specifically volunteered to do so. A representative of the Secret Service said this step had been necessary because the Service was "out of money.")

The reason for the impoverished condition of the Secret Service was evident—the appropriations committees were deadlocked that summer and no money could be spent by Congress. A representative of the Small Business Administra-

13. Huitt, "Congressional Organization in Money and Credit," p. 436.
14. *Congressional Quarterly Weekly Report*, June 22, 1962, p. 1062.

tion, which expected to receive $85–90 million from a dead-locked appropriations bill, said that the SBA had ceased making loans on March 9 in order to maintain a sufficient amount in its revolving fund to meet emergency requirements. As we have seen, State Department travel funds were also held up; ironically, congressmen themselves faced payday difficulties as the Legislative Appropriations bill was caught in the logjam.

A resolution passed by both houses in late June, which allowed government agencies to meet their financial commitments, was not an unmixed blessing. For agencies were permitted to continue only those projects *carried on in the expiring fiscal year*. This condition, of course, was an administrator's nightmare. No activity not carried on in fiscal 1962 could be funded. Left in abeyance were projects, such as the proposed U.S. pavilion at the New York World's Fair, which were to receive their first appropriation in the stranded Second Supplemental Appropriations Bill for fiscal 1963. This bill had been passed by both houses, but unfortunately, in different forms. Although the warring committees had made little attempt to iron out their basic differences, there had been attempts to rescue items in the Supplemental Appropriations bill. On June 14, the House passed a supplemental appropriation of $133,259,999. When the Senate raised the total to $277,222,429, the House refused to accept the higher figure. Once again, the representatives had passed a bill which the senators considered dangerously low and the upper chamber had countered with a measure which the House thought ridiculously high.

Included in the deadlocked bills were funds for the Agriculture Department's Marketing Service and Forest Service, Commerce's Coast and Geodetic Survey, HEW's Indian health activities, St. Elizabeth's hospital, and $80 million for grants to states—payments for prisoners, prison officials, and park services. More dramatic was the cutting off of new payments for the President's Disaster Relief Fund, to be used in storm-damaged areas. And especially disturbing to friends of education was the freezing of $15,707,000 of aid to federally "impacted" school districts—a sum which had been added by the Senate committee but which was now held up by the Senate–House appropriations deadlock.

For the administrators of the Secret Service, the Small Business Administration, and the Disaster Relief Fund, the appropriations battle was not at all humorous. Planning was crippled by financial uncertainty as the disruptive consequences of appropriations conflict became painfully evident.

Delay in governmental operations is not the only result of appropriations conflict which has drawn the attention of congressional observers. For reformers like Arthur Smithies[15] and George B. Galloway,[16] who would like Congress to consider the budget in a unified manner, conflict between the appropriations committees can only have harmful consequences. For such conflict is another fragmenting influence in Congressional consideration of the budget. Instead of working together to consider appropriations measures in the context of national economic goals, the Senate and House committees consider spending issues in the light of the prejudices of their own particular house of Congress.

DOES CONFLICT HAVE FUNCTIONS ALSO?

In the old days, the Senate listened only to appeals and didn't really inform itself in depth about appropriations. But that was before 1962. Cannon's charges pro-

15. Arthur Smithies, *The Budgetary Process in the United States* (New York, McGraw-Hill, 1955).

16. George B. Galloway, "Next Steps in Congressional Reform," University of Illinois Bulletin, *1* (1952).

voked us—all that he said about senators being spenders. Now the Senate committee is much more critical
of line-by-line expenditures.

Interviews indicated that, since 1962, senators and Senate
staff members were taking their appropriations work more
seriously. The staff assistant quoted above felt that Cannon's
bitter comments had been a "cutting edge" to the senators,
forcing them to justify appropriations by careful research
and closely reasoned arguments. Coser notes that "conflict
makes group members more conscious of their group bonds
and increases their participation."[17] Although this study was
carried out after 1962, and is therefore hampered in making
a comparison of committee behavior before and after the
feud, interviews did suggest that the Senate Appropriations
Committee members increased their participation in the
committee's work by more fully informing themselves about
the substance of appropriations legislation. This conclusion
must be tentative, but the possibility of a trend is still important. For insofar as intensified study of appropriations
measures by legislators is held to aid the budgetary process,
this result of conflict may be seen as beneficial to the governmental system.

If a function of theory is to illuminate certain relationships which exist in the real world, then it might be instructive to examine a few of Coser's propositions concerning
conflict to see what they can tell us about disruptions in the
appropriations process. Many of the theoretical relationships
were not readily apparent from a perusal of interview material, and few of them have been treated in the literature.
Nevertheless, the propositions are both interesting and deserving of further development.

For example, Coser discusses Simmel's statement that "out-

17. Coser, p. 90.

side conflict will strengthen the internal cohesion of the group."[18] Lack of pre-1962 interview data makes it difficult to gauge the effect of the battle on committee integration, but it appears that—at least for the staffs—the 1962 confrontation was a time of exhilarating group solidarity under the pressures of war. As we have seen, the tarnishing of the majority party and intervention by party leaders in the appropriations process made the feud quite unpleasant for many committee members. But the staffs did not view the prospect of future conflict with dismay.

Coser also notes that conflict may have the function of unifying diverse groups against a common enemy.[19] This unification, he asserts, might be beneficial to the groups and to the larger social system. Thus, our attention is directed to the contacts that were made between the Senate committee and the executive branch during the 1962 impasse. In the summer of that year, for instance, senators took a public stand in favor of increasing aid to schools in federally impacted areas. Working from a program mapped out by HEW's Office of Education, the Senate committee attempted to add $15,707,000 to the supplemental appropriations bill for the purpose of federal aid to education—but the House committee refused to go along. Increased legislative–executive cooperation in budgeting has long been a goal of reformers; in 1962 that goal was achieved when the Senate Appropriations Committee and the executive branch were compelled to join forces against the House committee to save specific programs.

Social theory points to still another way in which conflict may perform a function in the appropriations process: Coser says that "continued engagement in conflict tends to bring

18. Ibid., p. 88.
19. Ibid., p. 140.

about acceptance by both parties of common rules regulating the conduct of conflict . . . conflict also calls for a common organizational structure to facilitate the acceptance of common rules and conformity with them."[20] The 1962 battle was partially resolved when a modus vivendi was agreed upon for conducting further appropriations conferences: the meeting place would be located halfway between the two houses and the conference chairman would be selected by the subcommittee chairmen involved. Furthermore, a special committee, drawn from members of both houses, was created to review issues in the rift between the chambers. Therefore, a serious impasse did lead to the formulation of a set of rules to regulate the battle and also to the formation of a committee which would try to explore areas of possible agreement between the two bodies. Only time will tell how well the rules and the committee have served their purpose; appropriations conflict flared up again in the 1963 budgetary lag but there has been no major conflict since then. One may take the optimistic view that the 1962 fight was a device for "letting off steam" and releasing tensions between the two committees, to be followed by a consideration of issues and a calmer future relationship. But this view, as the 1963 clashes and 1964 interview comments indicate, might be a bit *too* optimistic. For harsh feelings still remain.

Finally, Coser notes that a social system split by various overlapping lines of opposition may be in less danger of being torn apart than a system which is split by only one major cleavage.[21] Thus, if party differences were the only ones that manifested themselves in Congress, there might be a breakdown in communication between one side and the other. But in the present case, Democrat–Republican lines

20. Ibid., p. 133.
21. Ibid., p. 76.

of division are neutralized by the opposition between House and Senate. If this opposition did not exist, Republicans and Democrats might not be as willing to cooperate with each other *within* the appropriations committees, thus causing a stalemate along party lines. Outside conflict encourages the working together and meshing of differentiated elements within the group.

Of course, a partisan stalemate might not occur if one party were strong and united enough to push an entire budget through Congress as a party measure. (A discussion of "party responsibility" will have to wait until the next chapter.) At any rate, it can be argued that conflict serves a purpose in a healthy system—acting out hostile feelings lets off steam and lessens the danger of more severe frustrations which might build up if all conflict were repressed.

If two prerequisites of rational budgetary planning are increased study of the measures by legislators and closer cooperation between the branches of government, then conflict in 1962 may have served some function. Furthermore, behavioral theories suggest that the appropriations battle did serve as an escape valve and resulted in the establishment of a set of procedures which offer hope for more amicable relations in the future. Finally, it might be held that the House–Senate cleavage is one of several rifts within Congress which prevent deep division along party lines and thus keep alive a spirit of bipartisan cooperation.

However, the fact does remain that the congressional "banana war" seriously impeded planning in several important agencies. Furthermore, the objections of reformers to the fragmenting influence of these battles must be dealt with. Many of the reform proposals might be unwise and many, while they are wise, might be politically impossible to effect. But that does not mean that the status quo must be maintained. Changes do take place, and it is important to understand when and why they do. Therefore, Chapter 6 will attempt to suggest some *preconditions* which must be satisfied before reform can be carried out, as well as to analyze the wisdom of various proposed changes in the budgetary system.

6

THE PRECONDITIONS OF REFORM

The assumption is that human institutions are tough and not easy to change.

Ralph Huitt[1]

The [appropriations] process has worked—so why don't we leave it alone?

Senate subcommittee chairman,
1964

Insistence on what are called realistic limits has always meant that they are assumed to be narrower and more rigid than they potentially are. History may be viewed as a process of pushing back walls of inevitability, of turning what have been thought to be inescapable limitations into human possibilities.

Helen M. Lynd[2]

Human institutions are not easy to change, and social scientists often show a marked reluctance to make the attempt. Bertram Gross provides an explanation for this reluctance:

> The reflective analyst is often so aware of the difficulties to be surmounted and so doubtful as to the adequacy of what he might propose that he stops short at description and critique . . . the idealist, finding out what some aspects of group life can be like, may come to the con-

1. Huitt, "Congressional Organization in Money and Credit," p. 406.
2. Helen M. Lynd, *On Shame and the Search for Identity* (New York, Harcourt, Brace and Company, 1958), p. 219.

clusion that all reform should be left to others who are more innocent about the stubborn realities . . . Finally, a negative approach may be expected from those whose standards lead them to endorse the *status quo* or accept it without challenge.[3]

The inadvisability of disrupting a "going concern" and the apparent political rigidity of congressional institutions are commonly taken as barriers to reform. Congress is doing its job, so why bother to change anything?

These arguments might be more appealing, were it not for the fact that history proves the nay-sayers wrong. Change is possible, and reform has left its mark on Congress. To those who felt that the number of standing committees could never be reduced, the Legislative Reorganization Act of 1946 came as a surprise. That act decreased the number of committees and clarified their jurisdiction. Furthermore, it reduced the huge load of private bills and increased the size of professional staffs. Finally, the Reorganization Act placed lobbying under tighter regulation. There was resistance to reform from powerful committees and interest groups, yet reform was accomplished. Even the House Rules Committee is not immune to change; its powers were limited at the beginning of the 1965 session by a coalition of liberal Democrats and like-thinking Republicans.

When a machine works imperfectly, we can at least make an attempt to fix it. House–Senate appropriations feuding stalled budgetary planning in 1949, 1961, and 1962; similar squabbling contributed to the 1963 appropriations lag. Because these conflicts tend to cause administrative distress, it is important to find some way to control the battles and to facilitate cooperation and communication between the two

3. Bertram M. Gross, *The Legislative Struggle* (New York, McGraw-Hill, 1953), pp. 451–52.

99

committees. Some clashing of ideas may be valuable and some decentralization of decision-making may be necessary, but long tieups of the budgetary process cause unusual discomfort in the executive branch. The problem is to prevent excessively damaging appropriations battles without losing the benefits of decentralization. Of course, the appropriations process is a working mechanism, and there is resistance to change within each house of Congress. But this does not mean that we must despair and then quickly surrender.

Rather, let us ask what the preconditions of appropriations reform are. What circumstances would facilitate changes in the budgetary process, changes which might mitigate the impact of feuds between the houses? Further, given the possibility of enactment of various reform proposals, how likely is each to contribute to the formation of sound public policy?

NATIONAL EMERGENCY

Congress is not, as a rule, very receptive to sweeping changes in procedure. But there are times when legislative lethargy is forced to give way to action. Because war and other national emergencies have, at various times in our history, caused congressmen to devise new, streamlined ways to meet old problems, we may list national emergency as one precondition of change in Congress. This is not to say that change can take place *only* in time of war; rather, wartime conditions produce new problems which demand rapid action.

In the days immediately preceding World War II, for example, a "Special Senate Committee Investigating the National Defense Program" was organized under the chairmanship of Senator Harry S. Truman.[4] The work of this

4. See Stephen K. Bailey and Howard D. Samuel, *Congress at Work* (New York, Henry Holt and Company, 1952), pp. 294–310.

committee, which extended into the wartime years, demonstrated the constructive way in which legislators may aid the nation during a time of peril. Assisted by a highly competent staff drawn from the executive branch, the Truman Committee surprised its critics by helping to make the war production effort more efficient. Hearings were thorough and responsible, and questions were carefully worded. The committee delved into many questions, e.g. aluminum shortages, ship construction, small business priorities, and troublesome labor disputes.

As representatives of the executive branch marched up to Capitol Hill to testify before the Truman Committee, observers noted the confidence that administrators had in the committee. The basis of this confidence was apparent: the legislators, who were all eager to bring defense contracts home to their districts, were nevertheless restraining themselves from strongly promoting their own local interests. Congressmen were changing their patterns of behavior to meet emergency conditions.

In its report, the Truman Committee sharply criticized President Roosevelt for his failure to more fully coordinate the process of war mobilization. The President, heeding the report, established the War Production Board—a powerful agency for coordinating the war effort on the home front. Because of its outstanding work, the committee had established itself as a congressional fixture and had proven that there was a place for continuous investigation of the defense program. The committee's early critics (including the *New York Times,* which had complained about the mediocre quality of the committee's legislators) were proved wrong.

National emergency has been a precondition for significant changes in general congressional procedure, but it is necessary for the purposes of this study to focus on the budgetary process in particular. Normally, little attempt is made to relate congressional action on revenues with action on expenditures. The House Ways and Means Committee, like the Appropriations Committee, is a proud and independent body—and the Ways and Means Committee has the final word on House tax decisions.

In the emergency conditions of 1950, the waging of the Korean War meant that expenditures would rise. Stimulated by the Joint Committee on the Economic Report, the Ways and Means Committee acted with unusual speed and efficiency to pass tax-increase measures in advance of expenditure increases. This proved to be a potent influence in stemming the tide of inflation in early 1951.[5] Because of the war, there was an unusual degree of cooperation between the taxing and spending committees in the House. Thus emergency conditions have served as a precondition of rapid and efficient congressional budgetary action.

We noted earlier that members of both appropriations committees have a common interest in the smooth working of the appropriations process. In times of emergency, the efficient operation of budgetary machinery becomes even more vital; the nation may be endangered by even a temporary stoppage of funds. Therefore, the common interest of appropriations committee members in the smooth working of the system becomes even stronger and the creation of some peacemaking machinery might become more likely. In a wartime situation it is conceivable that the House and Senate Appropriations Committees might join their staffs together in order to expedite the budgetary business at hand. Even if no structural changes grew out of the emergency conditions, it is probable that the committees would work together more closely than usual.

5. Arthur Smithies, *The Budgetary Process in the United States,* p. 137.

LEGISLATIVE ATTEMPTS TO COORDINATE APPROPRIATIONS: THE RECENT HISTORY

One way to reduce strife in appropriations politics might be to encourage cooperation among the two committees in formulating general budgetary policy. A plan along this line was the provision in the Legislative Reorganization Act of 1946 which called for the creation of a Joint Budgetary Committee with the duty of preparing a "legislative budget" and fixing a ceiling on the amount to be appropriated in a given year. The spending and taxing committees of each house were to meet at the beginning of the session to examine the President's budget and to report their legislative budget to Congress by February 15. Accompanying the report would be a joint resolution adopting it. (This plan would please both economizers, who wanted to hold down expenditures, and those reformers who wished to eliminate controversy between the committees.)

The legislative budget, which might have forced Congress to consider the overall effect of its fiscal actions, was not a success. In 1947 the joint resolution passed both houses but died in conference. The 1948 resolution also passed both houses but was ignored by Congress in making appropriations. In 1949 the deadline passed with no legislative budget forthcoming.[6] Still, as Huitt points out, the experience with the legislative budget cannot be taken as proof that all attempts at budgetary coordination will end in failure:

> In this case the machinery patently was defective. The four committees together were far too large a group to consider a budget. The time set as a deadline was too short. Moreover, it required the fixing of over-all totals

6. Huitt, pp. 441 ff., provides a good summary of recent reform efforts.

before the appropriations requests had even been considered.[7]

Another attempt at coordination was the employment of an omnibus appropriation bill in 1950. All spending measures for that year were consolidated into one bill. However, although Clarence Cannon supported the measure, the omnibus appropriations bill has not been tried again. Why was this plan abandoned? We noted earlier that in the House Appropriations Committee the subcommittees were the real centers of power. In 1950 Chairman Cannon appointed a special subcommittee of five to act as a clearing board for subcommittee bills. Following the screening, this special group would assemble a single bill for the full committee. Obviously, this procedure was anathema to the proud subcommittee chairmen who saw their leadership positions threatened by the new clearing committee. It would seem that any successful proposal must take into account the system of subcommittee autonomy and power which is so firmly entrenched in the House Appropriations Committee. Some form of representation must be offered to each subcommittee. The framers of the omnibus appropriations bill of 1950 did not recognize this power pattern; perhaps future reformers will be more careful.

THE JOINT COMMITTEE AS A DEVICE FOR REDUCING STRIFE

Before examining recent proposals for joint committees, we must first ask why the formation of a Joint Budgetary (or Appropriations) Committee would lead to better relations between the warring committees. If only a few members of each appropriations committee actually sat on a joint committee, and if the recommendations of the joint committee

7. Ibid., p. 441.

were not legally binding on its constituent elements, how could the formation of such a committee reduce tension between the antagonistic groups?

According to Boulding,

> the resolution of conflict depends on two factors—the reduction in the intensity of the conflict, on the one hand, and the development of overriding organizations which include both parties, on the other. Overriding organizations can develop . . . through the development of images in both parties in which there is acceptance of the role of a larger organization.[8]

If both appropriations committees were to send representatives to a joint committee, it is possible that the awareness of a common interest in the appropriations process as a whole would be strengthened on both sides. There might be more of a tendency for each committee to think of its counterpart in the other house as a partner, rather than as an antagonist, in the task of appropriating.

Furthermore, association in a cooperative venture might give rise to informal connections between the Senate and House committees which could carry over into conference work. Meeting together in a joint committee, senators and representatives would come to know each other better.

A Joint Budget Policy Committee: The Smithies Proposal

We now move to a consideration of specific joint committee proposals. The first plan examined was suggested by Arthur Smithies. Deploring the fragmentation of the budget in Congress, Smithies searches for a way to unify budgetary consideration. Programs, he feels, "should be considered and

8. Boulding, "Organization and Conflict," pp. 133–34.

appropriations made in broad terms—broad enough to permit unified consideration of the budget and to permit flexible administration in the Executive Branch."[9] Smithies proposes the creation of a Joint Budget Policy Committee of eighteen members, including the chairmen and ranking minority members of the House and Senate Appropriations Committees, the House Ways and Means Committee, and the Senate Finance Committee. Further, the committee would include the chairman, vice-chairman, and ranking minority members in the House and Senate of the Joint Committee on the Economic Report. Finally, there would be six members selected from Congress at large.[10]

The function of this committee, according to its proponent, would be first to consider the President's fiscal policies and to provide a framework for the later work of the appropriations and revenue committees. Then the committee would propose to Congress a concurrent resolution that embodied its findings with respect to appropriate budget policy. After the houses had adopted the concurrent resolution, the appropriations committees would pass an omnibus bill and would show that the appropriations proposed in that bill were in conformity with the Joint Committee's recommendations.

Smithies admits that such a plan is not likely to be accepted by Congress, and he is probably correct. In light of the omnibus bill experience in 1950, we can see that the Smithies proposal contains a fatal flaw: It does not recognize the power of the autonomous subcommittee chairmen of the House Appropriations Committee. These men would not agree to follow the recommendations of a committee in which they had no voice.

9. Smithies, p. 183.
10. Ibid., p. 192.

A Joint Appropriations Committee:
The McClellan Approach

Because Smithies' group includes members from so many committees, its creation would involve pacifying the taxing and spending committees, as well as the Joint Economic Committee. A less ambitious—and probably more realistic —proposal is embodied in a bill introduced by Senator John L. McClellan (D., Ark.) which has passed the Senate (but never the House) seven times. This bill would create a joint committee of fourteen members; seven from the Senate Appropriations Committee and seven from its counterpart in the House. Because this committee would be composed of appropriations legislators only, there would be no outcry against mixing the revenue and spending sides of the budget.

The essential function of this joint committee would be to provide a professional and nonpartisan staff of fiscal experts, who would make continuing budgetary studies of proposed and existing government programs. Following such a study, the staff would make relevant information available to congressmen. At the beginning of each session, the joint committee would report to the appropriations committees the total estimated costs of all previously authorized programs.[11]

11. John Saloma proposes a similar plan; his "Joint Committee on Fiscal Policy" would not be required to submit a formal legislative budget to Congress, but would exist primarily to provide an opportunity for congressional budgetary study. Although the increased information and interhouse communication to be gained from such a plan seem attractive, there are two criticisms which might be made of the proposal: First, by including taxing as well as spending committees, the jurisdictional problems are increased. Secondly, by limiting the size of the committee to 20, its proponent makes it unlikely that each House subcommittee will be sufficiently represented. (See Saloma, *The Responsible Use of Power*, pp. 75–77.)

Unfortunately, McClellan's proposal runs into the same roadblock that Smithies' does. There are places for seven senators and seven representatives on the McClellan committee; however, there are thirteen Senate subcommittees and twelve House subcommittees. Unless each House subcommittee is represented on a joint committee, the proposals of the latter group might be ignored—at least by those subcommittees not represented. Perhaps McClellan's proposed committee could be enlarged to include a representative from each House subcommittee.

At any rate, the McClellan bill may have a chance for passage. After all, it was said at one time that the House Ways and Means Committee would never share its taxing power. Yet today there exists a Joint Committee on Internal Revenue Taxation, made up of ranking members of the Senate and House taxing committees. Serving both the Senate Finance and House Ways and Means Committees, the joint staff is the chief reason for the committee's existence. And the staff has been able to provide professional information to both parent committees. (Of course, the House Appropriations Committee, with its autonomous subcommittees, will be a tougher nut to crack than was Ways and Means. But the experience of the Joint Committee on Internal Revenue Taxation shows us that House–Senate staff sharing is possible.)

During the 1964 interviews, legislators were asked for their opinions on the proposed joint appropriations committee. One liberal on the House committee remarked that "a Joint Committee on the Budget is no good. Joint committees tend to destroy the concept of the Founding Fathers." That "concept" was a bicameral legislature. Another House committee member added that "all it [a joint committee] would do is add another layer of staff and not contribute anything."

These views are fairly typical of those held by House committee members. Surprisingly, the joint committee idea also ran into some opposition in the Senate, although 77 members had cosponsored the McClellan bill in the 88th Congress. Even one sponsor of the joint committee bill went so far as to say: "I would not recommend a Joint Committee on Appropriations."

Although there is opposition to the idea of a Joint Appropriations Committee, there is also support for it in both houses of Congress, stronger, as might be expected, in the Senate than in the House. However, one rising House committee member remarked:

> I would favor a Joint Appropriations Committee . . . A joint committee would save time with agencies downtown. Appropriations bills would be passed earlier . . . Also, a joint committee would have a better idea of what budgetary requirements were . . . It is long in the future, but someday we'll get to it. In about twenty years, we'll approve a joint committee.

How could a joint committee proposal pass Congress and, after passage, be successfully implemented in the appropriations system?

Writers like Smithies and Galloway[12] have campaigned for more party discipline in Congress, as a path toward unified consideration of the budget. In attacking Smithies' proposal, Wildavsky asserts that no party is strong enough to carry a budget through Congress:

> There is no cohesive group in Congress capable of using these devices to affect decision-making by imposing its preferences on a majority of Congressmen. Smithies' budgetary reform presupposes a completely different

12. Galloway, "Next Steps in Congressional Reform."

political system from the one that exists in the United States. To be sure, there is a name for a committee that imposes its will on the legislature and tolerates no rival committees—it is called a Cabinet on the British model.[13]

The assumption, then, has been that the American system does not include parties strong enough to enforce compliance with the recommendations of a Joint Budgetary Committee or a Joint Appropriations Committee. Another assumption —presented by Smithies—is that if a party *could* successfully enforce compliance, then the resulting unification of the budgetary process would necessarily contribute to the formulation of rational public policy. This study will examine both assumptions carefully, asking two questions: Is an American majority party, backed by a President, strong enough to enforce the recommendations of a Joint Budgetary Committee? Even if it were possible to unify the budgetary process, would such unification be beneficial for public policy?

THE ROLE OF THE PARTY

Discussing the House Appropriations Committee, Fenno says that "one need only examine the conditions most likely to decrease committee integration to ascertain some of the critical factors for producing changes in the appropriations process."[14] As we have seen in Chapter 3, House committee integration is based on nonpartisanship. If partisan considerations were to come to the fore in the minds of the congressmen, integration would be greatly weakened.

House committee integration and the resistance of the proud and independent subcommittees have been the chief

13. Wildavsky, *The Politics of the Budgetary Process*, p. 133.
14. Fenno, "House Appropriations Committee," p. 324.

obstacles to the formation of a joint committee. Therefore, if one wants to influence a legislator, he must place a demand on the congressman in such a way as to break that man's sub-committee tie. The reward offered a congressman for "going along" with the joint committee and its recommendations must be more important to the legislator than continued adherence to subcommittee norms which militate against acceptance of the joint committee idea. Since a congressman's first need is reelection, and since his party may influence—to a certain extent—his reelection chances, the party is the logical instrument with which to press reform. If the party can convince a congressman that his chances for reelection will be diminished if he does not "cooperate" in the stream-lining of the budgetary process, then the reform may well be possible.

But why would a majority party want to have a Joint Appropriations Committee in the first place? If a President of the opposite party were in power, a majority party might want to use a joint committee to present a coherent alternative to the presidential budget. On the other hand, if the President were of the majority party, the congressional leadership could take advantage of the joint committee machinery to facilitate rapid passage of the presidential budget.

Since conflict between House and Senate may embarrass the majority leadership, as it did in 1962, and because a breakdown in the spending process delays enactment of the President's budget, a majority party is likely to be receptive to proposals designed to moderate such clashes. In 1962 Senate Majority Leader Mansfield declared that "the interest of the entire Congress and the nation would be served"[15] by a cessation of hostilities between the warring committees.

15. *Congressional Quarterly Weekly Report,* June 29, 1962, p. 1087.

A major political party might well decide to support a joint committee proposal in order to make open breaks less likely. Given the desire of a party to support a joint committee, how can that party make its demands felt by recalcitrant legislators?

"Party Government Is Impossible Here"

As we have seen, there are two basic preconditions for the creation and successful functioning of a Joint Budgetary Committee or a Joint Appropriations Committee:

1. A majority party (preferably aided by the leverage of presidential support) would have to commit itself to the joint committee proposal.

2. The party would have to persuade uncooperative legislators to go along with the proposal. Specifically, the party would have to demonstrate to House Appropriations Committee members that it would be more costly for them to ignore the party's "advice" than to break precious subcommittee norms which militate against reform.

Even if the first precondition is satisfied, observers[16] feel that a party is really powerless to force its joint committee plans upon disagreeing congressmen. Smithies indicates that his proposal would be impractical without a marked strengthening of party discipline. And Huitt agrees—although he notes the work of Truman[17] and Turner[18] on the impor-

16. E.g. Huitt, Wildavsky.
17. David B. Truman, *The Congressional Party: A Case Study* (New York, John Wiley & Sons, 1959).
18. Julius Turner, *Party and Constituency: Pressures on Congress* (Baltimore, The Johns Hopkins Press, 1951).

tance of the party in influencing congressional voting decisions.

Those who are skeptical of the possibility of party government say that, in the United States, candidates for Congress are elected on the basis of local considerations. Because the national party plays a relatively small part in local congressional races, it is unable to make its demands for budgetary reform meaningful to the legislator. As Huitt remarks:

> The member of Congress ... is almost surely self-selected ... where organizational approval *is* mandatory, adherence to some national policy probably would be the last test to be applied ... In his campaign for election [the candidate] may wrap himself in his party's mantle or virtually ignore it, or indeed he may even embrace the views of the other side.[19]

Staggered terms of office have been cited as one factor which makes "real party government impossible in the United States."[20] Other obstacles suggested are the federal system, the separation of powers, and the lack of intraparty unity.

Rather than accepting on faith the existence of these obstacles, the political scientist has an obligation to ask whether these barriers prevent a party from influencing a congressman's election chances and, if so, how they can be overcome. President Johnson's proposal that House members serve four-year terms, coincident with those of the President, would certainly make staggered elections a less formidable obstacle to party government. Even without this change, there is evidence that the hurdle is far from an insuperable one. Irwin N. Gertzog has examined this question in depth,

19. Huitt, p. 410.

20. E. E. Schattschneider, *Party Government* (New York, Rinehart and Company, 1942), p. 126.

and his results are instructive for a discussion of the power of parties.[21] Noting the evidence presented by Stokes and Miller,[22] which suggests that midterm voters are even more likely to be party-oriented than those who vote in presidential years, Gertzog undertakes a study of midterm electoral behavior.

Describing the midterm campaign activities of Presidents from Wilson to Kennedy, Gertzog notes that each Chief Executive since Franklin Roosevelt campaigned more vigorously than did his immediate predecessor. (Even if a President is not on the campaign trail, his actions as Chief Executive can exert a marked influence on the voting. Truman's ending of price controls and statements advocating the admittance of Jewish refugees to Palestine were helpful to the Democratic cause in 1946.) Cabinet members have also taken increasingly to the campaign trail; because of the enlarged role of the federal government in foreign and domestic affairs, officials in the executive branch are often dealing with issues that concern voters at the grass roots.

In 1962, President Kennedy used his influence and control of the party apparatus to elect men who were willing to help him pass bills on medical care for the aged, aid to education, and mass transit. As Gertzog's statistics show, presidential influence may have been decisive in a number of cases.[23] If, say, President Johnson and the Democratic Party were to commit themselves to budgetary reform in a future election year, who could maintain that congressmen would not take notice?

21. Irwin N. Gertzog, "The Role of the President in the Midterm Congressional Election" (Ph.D. dissertation, University of North Carolina, 1965).

22. Donald E. Stokes and Warren E. Miller, "Party Government and the Saliency of Congress," *Public Opinion Quarterly*, 26 (Winter 1962), 531–46.

23. Gertzog, p. 242.

In his summation, Gertzog suggests that midterm elections for the House of Representatives do not constitute a serious obstacle to party government. Presidential incumbents act "as if there was a substantial difference in the programs and policies espoused by the two parties and have asked the electorate to return a majority of congressmen who, at least by implication, would be sympathetic to the Administration's legislative measures." And an overwhelming number of voters have cast ballots for the candidate with whose party they identified. Gertzog therefore concludes that:

> when voters continue to be guided by considerations of party label, and when an incumbent President takes an active and positive campaign role, even though he himself is not on the ballot, both behave *as if* party government existed in this country. Thus, if and when other deterrents to the integration of party government are overcome, midterm political practices . . . stand ready to facilitate, not retard, that integration.[24]

The "other deterrents" to the integration of party government are less formal elements like disunity on matters of public policy. If internal disunity were decreased, the recommendations of a Joint Appropriations Committee or a Joint Budgetary Committee would have clearer sailing. Gertzog's work is valuable in pointing out flaws in the argument that the party and Administration can exert but limited influence on congressional races.

It appears, then, that our second precondition for the formation and support of a Joint Budgetary Committee has at least a chance of being fulfilled. Led by a strong President, a party could make the creation of such a committee a key element of policy which legislators could ignore only at the risk of losing electoral support. Members of the House Ap-

24. Ibid., pp. 258–59.

propriations subcommittees, who represent the chief obstacle to reform, would not be immune from this kind of electoral pressure. Thus, the party leadership could break down resistance to the plan by making party demands more salient to legislators than the norms of subcommittee unity.

If the creation and support of a Joint Budgetary Committee is judged to be a political possibility (assuming the necessary preconditions of party interest and party power), we must consider whether such a committee would in fact aid the development of constructive public policy.

Before we can examine the policy consequences of joint committee decisions, we must distinguish between the various kinds of joint committees proposed. Tom Wicker, for example, spoke of a Joint Appropriations Committee which would consist of the two separate appropriations committees welded into one. Smithies advocates the creation of a Joint Budgetary Committee whose recommendations would be incorporated into a concurrent resolution and an omnibus appropriations bill. Finally, the McClellan proposal envisages a joint committee made up of seven members from each of the presently existing appropriations committees. However, the functions of this committee would be merely to supervise staff investigations of budgetary problems and to provide information to legislators; the McClellan committee would not seek to dictate budgetary policy by means of a concurrent resolution.

Because the Wicker and Smithies joint committee proposals attempt to centralize budgetary decision-making in a single group of men, they could be attacked by incrementalists on the grounds that such centralization makes compromise less likely. For it is much more difficult to reach agreement on basic budgetary plans than on smaller, fragmented issues. Instead of expediting the process, the joint committee might be stalled indefinitely over a policy dispute.

Furthermore, incrementalists would argue that, because of the limits of human comprehension, the individual joint committee member would be unable to examine the entire budget in a careful manner. The Smithies proposal, because it contains a provision for an omnibus appropriations measure, would be vulnerable also to the charge that it places an enormous burden on the congressman who would have to vote on the appropriations bill. For he would be confronted by an enormous package late in the session and would have had little foreknowledge of individual items. Fragmentation is a necessary aid to calculation. (However, let us not confuse incrementalism as a description of what actually happens in congressional practice with a dogmatic statement of what *ought* to happen. It is arguable that a joint committee staff could provide a legislator with information which would enable him to take a more comprehensive view of the budget.)

The effective representation of interests is a further problem for Smithies' committee. As we have seen, the existence of two distinct appropriations committees provides both economizers and spenders with recognized champions in the budgetary arena. Because it multiplies the points of access to influence and power, a fragmented appropriations system is sensitive to political demands in many sectors of society.

Under a joint committee system in which a single committee could make fundamental budgetary decisions, the number of points of access to influence would be decreased. The economizers would lose the independent voice of the budget-slashing House Appropriations Committee. On the other side, the executive branch agencies would be denied their "special relationship" with a strong Senate committee. The joint committee would thus have a difficult time determining the intensity with which values were held in the relevant groups, and many of those groups would feel cut off from the centers of budgetary power.

If a major task of democratic government is to record the values held in society and to provide access to power for the various segments of the populace, then the creation of a strong Joint Budgetary Committee along the lines suggested by Smithies is open to criticism. Although it might (by encouraging cooperation between Senate and House) decrease the possibility of open breaks between the houses, it is not at all clear that this kind of joint committee would aid budgetary calculation, compromise, or representation.

But what about the McClellan committee? Is that proposal open to the same objections? To be sure, there are criticisms of the McClellan bill. "The McClellan proposal is anathema. If we're going to have two houses, let's have two houses." This comment of a junior member of the House committee reflects House unwillingness to cooperate with the Senate in any joint venture. Still, because the McClellan proposal (unlike that put forward by Smithies) does not centralize basic appropriations planning, does not provide for dictation of policy to the two appropriations committees, and does not include an omnibus appropriations bill, it cannot be dismissed on the same grounds as the Smithies plan. The McClellan committee is primarily an *information-gathering* body; it permits the two appropriations committees to remain autonomous bodies with power intact. Thus, both economizers and government bureaus are left with their routes of access to power unimpaired. If the McClellan proposal provided for adequate subcommittee representation, all would be well. As we have seen, its failure to do so constitutes the major flaw of this plan.

118

Discussing budgetary reform, Wildavsky declares:

> It is not too much to suggest that a lot of reform be preceded by a little knowledge. Until we develop a more adequate description of budgeting, until we know something about the "existential situation" in which the participants find themselves under our political system, proposals for major reform must be based on woefully inadequate understanding.[25]

Certainly, any reform proposal must take into account the power relationships that exist between participants in the appropriations process. Specifically, reform must be predicated upon a recognition of these elements of the "existential situation":

1. Power in the House Appropriations Committee rests in the twelve powerful subcommittees which make up the group. This fact was recognized in 1962, when negotiations for an end to the budgetary dispute were left in the hands of the subcommittee pairs involved. But it is *not* recognized by those who call for an omnibus appropriations bill or who advocate the creation of a joint committee which does not represent all subcommittee groups. (Although one man may sit on more than one subcommittee, the strong principle of subcommittee independence would make it difficult for a congressman to represent two or three subcommittees at once.) A workable reform proposal must offer representation of some kind to each subcommittee group.

25. Wildavsky, p. 144.

2. Because the existence of two separate appropriations committees provides both spenders and economizers with access to governmental power and provides legislators with vital information about group demands, a reform proposal which concentrates the basic decision-making in one body runs the risk of depriving important groups of the feeling that they are being represented.

3. Open battles between the two appropriations committees that tie up the budgetary process make planning difficult for executive branch administrators who find their agencies cut off from funds. Even an emergency continuing resolution does not solve an agency's problems, for no new projects may be initiated under such a resolution. In an era of rapid technological change, a prohibition against the initiation of new programs is stifling indeed.

During the interviews, members of both the Senate and House committees expressed their feeling that the size of the professional appropriations staffs should be increased. A Republican House committee member remarked: "The appropriations process is *not* working well. We're at a disadvantage . . . We don't have sufficient staff to check into the post office and find out if they're efficient." On the other side of Congress, a Democratic senator noted that "the fault of Congress lies in not having a skilled group of auditors. We handle a big budget on conversation."[26]

Is there a way to accommodate the demand for a larger, technically competent staff and, at the same time, satisfy those who desire to moderate House–Senate conflict? We

26. Saloma, pp. 45 ff., discusses the arguments pro and con increased staffing. In the end, he comes out for an increase in the number of professional staff members.

have seen that staff members serve important functions in the appropriations process: they prepare the statistics and program evaluations that form the bases of congressmen's decisions on how much to appropriate. Interviews indicated that the staff aides, because of their fierce devotion to the committees on which they serve, increase the cohesion of these committees and strengthen the groups' ideologies. Because the House and Senate committees' ideologies both include an element of hostility toward the opposite group, zealous staff members are led to accentuate the differences between the committees and thus make compromise less likely.

Since the professional staff members are so vital an element in the process, reformers should investigate ways of utilizing staff to prevent conflict. A step in this direction might be the creation of a *conference committee staff,* composed of experts in various fields who would not be loyal specifically to one committee or the other. Rather, these professionals would be charged with preparing for the work of the conference committees by studying the differences in House and Senate bills and by doing independent research into the subject matter involved. The special staff members would help to arbitrate disputes by suggesting mutually beneficial routes to compromise.

Could this staff be designed in such a way as to deal with the fact of subcommittee independence within the House committee? The answer here might be to include in the conference staff an expert in each of the separate fields covered by the subcommittees.[27] Each man would work for a different pair of subcommittees, his function being to conduct specialized research in his area of competence and to

27. Agriculture; Defense; D.C.; Foreign Operations; Independent Offices; Interior; Labor–HEW; Legislative; Military Construction; Public Works; State, Justice, Commerce, and Judiciary; Treasury–Post Office.

aid both the Senate and House subcommittees working in that area. A conference staff might be integrated into a joint committee staff. Such a plan would have the double merit of providing full-time informational work for the conference staff and also offering representation to each appropriations subcommittee on the joint committee staff.

This proposal would not—as would the Smithies suggestion—decrease the points of access to power for economizers and bureau chiefs by centralizing basic appropriations decision-making in one body. Like the McClellan proposal, the conference staff plan would leave the basic budgetary decisions in the places where they now reside: the separate Senate and House committees and subcommittees. However, the proposal differs from McClellan in that it treats the House subcommittees as the powerful independent bodies that they are.

Now we must ask whether the conference staff would increase the possibilities for cooperation between the House and Senate Appropriations Committees. Schelling notes that "The 'obvious' outcome [of bargaining] depends greatly on how the problem is formulated, on what analogies or precedents the definition of the bargaining issue calls to mind, on the kinds of data that may be available to bear on the questions in dispute."[28] Because members of the conference staff would be charged with familiarizing themselves with each subcommittee's bill and then with formulating the data for conference consideration, they would be in a unique position to suggest certain "obvious" outcomes which might be acceptable to both sides.

Furthermore, the conference committee staff would serve as a reminder to appropriations congressmen that there is considerable feeling both on Capitol Hill and in the nation

28. Schelling, *The Strategy of Conflict*, p. 69.

at large that appropriations conflicts should be avoided. By reminding the congressmen of their common interest in the maintenance of a speedy and efficient appropriations process, the conference staff could help to fashion compromise in areas where the interests of the two committees diverge.

Finally, the conference staff might make the warring committees susceptible to what has been called the process of "social contagion."[29] Forced to take the small step of sharing a staff with a would-be opponent, members of a House subcommittee would have to justify this move to themselves. Thus they might be forced to (1) take account of some of the good qualities of their rivals, (2) minimize the hostile intentions of their adversaries, and (3) predict that the positive approach of sharing a staff would be more successful than continued non-communication and non-cooperation.

It appears, therefore, that a conference committee staff—possibly included as part of a joint committee staff—fulfills our three necessary conditions for reform. It offers representation to each House subcommittee unit, it maintains multiple routes of access to power in the appropriations system, and it acts to minimize prolonged strife in the appropriations process.

Whether such a measure would pass in Congress depends largely upon the ability of a majority party (if possible, backed by the President) to make its demands more meaningful to a congressman than the dictates of his House Appropriations subcommittee. A President and party that made appropriations reform part of their legislative agenda could threaten to withhold electoral support from those who refused to go along. Because the Appropriations Committee shapes House attitudes on matters in this field, the end of

29. See Irving Janis and Daniel Katz in *Journal of Conflict Resolution,* *1* (June 1957), 94.

committee resistance would probably mean the end of House resistance.

A further problem might arise in integrating the conference staff with the two existing appropriations staffs. How do we know that the present staffs will share information with the new one? To meet this problem, it is essential to select for the new group men with unusual competence in their particular fields. If they can offer valuable specialized advice to the appropriations committees, their integration will be made easier.

INCREMENTAL CHANGE

Even if no structural reform is made in the appropriations process, incremental changes will continue to be carried out within the present structure. These changes will be most likely to come when (1) important party measures are being blocked by appropriations subcommittees (thus the Eisenhower Administration worked in subcommittee to break down Republican resistance to foreign aid) and (2) party demands are most meaningful to legislators (as in election years). As we have seen, Chairman George Mahon effected incremental change when he applied pressure to force the passage of a party measure (foreign aid) in an election year (1964). This action did represent a change in appropriations procedure, for Mahon had to overrule Foreign Operations subcommittee chairman Passman in order to bring about the desired result. In 1965 Mahon took the next step in incremental change when he reshuffled Passman's subcommittee to give that body a more liberal hue.

On March 9, 1965, the Senate adopted by a vote of 88–0 a concurrent resolution to establish a joint congressional committee to study the organization and operation of Congress. The House concluded legislative action on the proposal by passing the concurrent resolution on March 11 by voice vote. Senator A. S. Mike Monroney (D., Okla.), sponsor of the resolution and subsequently appointed as a co-chairman of the joint committee, said that the committee could do valuable work "in studying such areas as improved methods for Congress to handle federal spending proposals."[30]

Bertram Gross has noted:

> Proposals for change in the legislative process are much like legislative bills in that their chances of success depend upon the campaigns waged for and against them. No idea for improvement in the legislative process can have any effect unless it seems attractive enough to have a campaign built around it and unless there are people who develop this campaign.[31]

If a campaign were needed to press for appropriations reform, the Joint Committee on the Organization of Congress was a body which could start the movement rolling. From May to September 1965, the Committee heard suggestions for reform from senators, representatives, political scientists, and interest group representatives. The House–Senate appropriations conflict was still a live issue; Co-chairman Monroney wondered:

> What kind of mediation board can we have to resolve these disagreements between the two Houses . . . after this committee ceases to exist, you see, then there must be some continuing body that will be there to mediate so we will not be tied up, as we were a couple of years ago on Christmas eve on failure to get appropriations to conference committees.[32]

30. *Congressional Quarterly Weekly Report*, March 12, 1965, p. 376.

31. Gross, pp. 452–53.

32. Joint Committee on the Organization of Congress, *Hearings* (89th Cong., 1st Sess., 1965), p. 59.

Referring in his testimony to "the breakdown in our appropriations procedure which occurred during the 87th Congress, and which is a matter of the greatest concern to all of us,"[33] Senator McClellan defended his joint committee proposal as a path toward cooperation and harmony between the appropriations committees. Testifying in support of McClellan's bill were five representatives and three senators.[34]

One important part of McClellan's bill is Section 3, which authorizes the joint committee to recommend joint hearings by the House and Senate appropriations subcommittees—in order to expedite the process and save wear and tear on harried Administration officials. Even if formal joint committee legislation is not enacted, it is possible that joint appropriations hearings may be held for reasons of convenience. Such hearings would necessitate cooperation between Senate and House staffs in making preliminary arrangements and between subcommittee chairmen in conducting the meetings. Cooperation here might lead to harmony in conference.

At any rate, the 1965 hearings demonstrated that legislators were concerned about the possibility of further appropriations feuding and were thinking constructively about methods of preventing it. This is not surprising, for both senators and representatives have something to gain from the prevention of strife in the appropriations process. For fiscal conservatives, the absence of interhouse warfare would mean that congressional budgetary specialists would be free to devote their full energies to an examination of financial measures proposed by the executive branch. Especially if aided by an expert staff, these specialists could exert a prudent control on federal spending. For a liberal majority party

33. Ibid., p. 477.
34. Representatives Dorn, Halpern, Lindsay, McClory, Rumsfeld, Senators Clark, Moss, Saltonstall.

backed by a friendly White House, the speeding of appropriations legislation would make it possible for the President's social welfare projects to be promptly initiated and confidently administered. For all members of Congress, the decrease in House–Senate conflict would raise the prestige of the national legislature.

Human institutions are rigid, and they are not easy to change. But this is not a sufficient reason for surrendering the quest for solutions to political problems. If the appropriations process has worked tolerably well in the past, there is no reason why it cannot be made to work still better in the future.

INDEX

Italicized page numbers refer to tabular material.